GW00501479

A TIMELESS WORLD

Edited by

Heather Killingray

First published in Great Britain in 2002 by
POETRY NOW
Remus House,
Coltsfoot Drive,
Peterborough, PE2 9JX
Telephone (01733) 898101
Fax (01733) 313524

All Rights Reserved

Copyright Contributors 2002

HB ISBN 0 75434 377 4
SB ISBN 0 75434 378 2

FOREWORD

Although we are a nation of poets we are accused of not reading poetry, or buying poetry books. After many years of listening to the incessant gripes of poetry publishers, I can only assume that the books they publish, in general, are books that most people do not want to read.

Poetry should not be obscure, introverted, and as cryptic as a crossword puzzle: it is the poet's duty to reach out and embrace the world.

The world owes the poet nothing and we should not be expected to dig and delve into a rambling discourse searching for some inner meaning.

The reason we write poetry (and almost all of us do) is because we want to communicate: an ideal; an idea; or a specific feeling. Poetry is as essential in communication, as a letter; a radio; a telephone, and the main criterion for selecting the poems in this anthology is very simple: they communicate.

CONTENTS

Swan	A F Brown	1
Not Today	Simon P Jones	1
Winter Memories	J Harper-Smith	2
Renaissance	Gerard Allardyce	2
Night Demons	Jerome Kiel	3
The Sunny Hours	Roma Davies	4
Stubborn Path	V Topp	4
Soulmates	Carlamarie Haynes	5
Jazz	Angus Richmond	6
The Waterfall	Joe Baird	6
The Good Life?	Frank Angel	7
A Gypsy's Last Goodbye	Joyce Healy	8
Sun Rising	Colin Zarhett	8
Third Time Lucky	Catherine Keepin	9
What Is It?	Carole A Smith	10
Renewal	N Lord	11
Miscry	A Barrett	12
Waiting	Robert Dell	12
The Valley Of The Shadow	Flora Hughes	13
Have A Drink On Me Rose	M Vukasinovic	13
Sergeant Pepper Ends The Empire	P Ardern	14
Warrior	Ian Barton	15
Routines	Audrey Petersen	16
Tae The Bard - Rabbie	Sylvia Gold	18
Sharing And Caring	I M Stead	19
How To Trick A Know-It-All	Pam Iwantschak	20
Adventure	Michael Courtney Soper	20
Words For Reminders	Viv Lionel Borer	21
Ed-You-Cayshun	John Troughton	22
Just A Game	H Cotterill	23
I And My Dog	R B Manning	24
A Little While	Barbara Crick	24
Pictures On My Mind	Dawn P Dodd	25
Family Ties	Hilda Ellis	25
Us	Roger Mather	26

Red Wall	Paul Willis	27
Barbed Wire	Dawn Marshallsay	28
Gift Of A Single Rose	Mary Morley	29
A Wish	Muriel Willa	30
Love For A Dog	Laura Somerville	30
An Alien	Jean Roberts	31
Chosen	Heather Ann Breadnam	32
Posters	Peter Asher	33
How Can You?	Ken Mills	34
Man's Folly	A J Lawrence	34
The Master Artist	Funmilayo Ojedokun	35
Adam's Rib	John Ball	35
The Surgery	Kevin Michael Jones	36
But Where Do I Go From Here?	Christala Rosina	37
The Military Parade	Bill Drayton	38
Radiating	Daniel White	38
Shy Only With You!	Hacene Rahmouni	39
By Long	Lisha Naomi Binns	39
My Thoughts Of The World Today	Peter Antonian	40
To Freedom	Sybil Curzon	40
Can't Think, Won't Think	Anne Boyd	41
The Music Of Life	Kathleen Fox-Watson	41
Thank You, I Know	Lynsey Stopforth	42
Untitled	Sheri-Lynne Dike-Johns	42
No Regrets	Olive Portsmouth	43
Life Or Death	Wayne Cotter	43
New Beginnings	Kayleigh Jones	44
A Beautiful Mind	Chris T Barber	44
Were You There?	Rosemary Peach	45
Glasses	E Kelly	46
The Golden Jubilee	D M Carne	46
Pictures In My Mind	Jonathan Pegg	47
The Mirror Of Life	Doris Shaw	48
The Silent Seducer	Harry M M Walker	49
Life's Pilgrimage	Joyce Allan	50
11th September 2001	Joyce Lawrence	51
When I Am Gone	Pamela R Dalton	52

Wish You Were Here	S Glover	53
What's Real	Rodney Epstein	53
Hate	Carman	54
Falling Star	Niresha Umaichelvam	54
Life	Helen Davis	55
Scene Of Crime	C Karalius	56
Joy Of Laughter	Joan Hands	56
The Caged Bird	S Zartashia Al-Jalaly	57
Year Round	Pettr Manson-Herrod	57
Broken Dreams	David Russell	58
The Skylark	J B Vanson	58
Mum - A Little Word With A Huge Meaning	S G Williams	59
To Ascot	P Evans	60
Leave Me Be	Lorna Marlow	61
The Deceiver	Paddy Jupp	62
Love On The Rocks - With A Twist	Brenda Conn	62
A Mother's Work	Robertine Muriel	63
Why?	Lynda Hopkinson	63
Wedding Song	Oliver R Howells	64
The Lady That Dances	Carole A Cleverdon	64
Piano And Sunsets	Carol Ann Darling	65
Bitter Lemon	Alex Swift	66
The Beauty Of Willen Lake	Christine Barrow	67
Gren	Abbie Durrant	68
It's Wonderful Thing	Dorothy Marshall Bowen	69
The One And Only Source	Zoë L Mitchell	70
Wendy	Gloria Thorne	71
Saturday	Sylvia Bareham	72
Violence And Crime	Una Chandler	72
Aliens Among Us	Pamela Evans	73
My Inner Child	Tina Reeks	74
Render Well	Hugh Campbell	75
All Is Well	Roseline T Chirape	76
Your Secret's Safe	Paula Puddephatt	77
Dovecote	Lyn Peacock-Sayers	78
Requescant In Pace	Carmel Lynch	78

Madness Squared	Paul Stevenson	79
Round The World	Sylvester Espana	80
Big Now	Alex Dickie	80
A Draft Of Shadows	Joe Loxton	81
Cerebral Celebration	Michael Bell	82
Frustration	Olive L Groom	83
Ploughing A Furrow In The Fields Of Misery	James Gibbons	84
Last Night	E J James	84
Food For Thought	Ivor Emlyn Percival	85
A Day At The Zoo	Julie Hampson	86
The Quiet Tree	Dorothy C Blakeman	87
Today I Will!	Wendy-Elezabeth Smith	88
Memory Of The Queen Mother	Andrew Bray	89
An April Wedding	John Walmsley	90
Merely A Player	Helen Bulford	91
Nemesis	S A List	92
A Freedom 'Hero'	Ron Wakely	92
Untitled	B T Bell	93
Poem	June Hill	93
Listening	Talbot Tully	94
Lost Voices	June Fox	95
Tranquillity	Patrick Morrissey	96
A Garden Full Of Roses	Florence Hall	97
Rain	Elizabeth Millington	98
The Loss Of A Trawler	Ronald Blay	99
Play Me	Alexa Raisbeck	100
The Drum	Mike Tinsley	100
Lost Child	Grace McGregor	101
A Friend	Emma Tagg	102
I Am Blessed	Gavin Clements	103
Kingston	Kenneth Kirby	104
Kite-Flying	Brian Garfield	105
More Than Words	Lisa Parris	106
Santorini	Joan Sculpher	108
Reconciliation	Margaret Roach	108
Once I Was Young	Derek J Morgan	109
Pocket Stone	Matthew Goodyear	110

A Country Lane	Kinsman Clive	110
Dementia Dreaming	J M Gardener	111
Loneliness	Adam Russell	112
What Do We Want?	Chris Buxton	112
The Blackbird	Pamela Rollin	113
Day Out	Annie Harris	114
Hope	Martin Hackett	114
Politics	A W Day	115
To Love Someone	Sharon McHugh	116
Mourning After Thrills	Karishma Brahmbhatt	116
He'll Be There	E B Holcombe	117
Hatred	Nigel J Mason	117
Escape	Andy Sweet	118
Thanatos And Eros	P Hughes-Wilson	119
Youth's Lament	Catherine L Woodward	120
Untitled	Maxene Huntley	121
Memory	Margaret King	122
Waterfall Of Tears	Michael Spittles	122
One Afternoon	Heather Moore	123
Untitled	Chris Lodge	123
Heritage Rap	Stephen Bonney	124
Wind On The Water	Dean Juniper	124
Senior Members	Michiko Matthews	125
The Piano	Mickey Gough	126
Après Un Rêve	Pam Love	127
The Year Of Our Lord - 2002	Opal Innsbruk	128
The Windy Precipice	Denise Startin	129
Who'd Feed The Cats?	Lindsey Susan Powell	130
Slightly Different, But Still Just Another Christmas	Karen Eberhardt Shelton	131
Beyond The Hairstyle	Stella Durand	132
Anchor Free	Constance Roper	132
Alone	J Redfearn	133
Father	Dawn Voice-Cooper	133
From Where?	Susan Barker	134
Elusive Ballerina	Sarah A O'Leary	135
Dark Cloud	Philip Gustard	136
Bedtime With Dad	K Baldwin	137

Thor	David M Garnett	138
The Fish	Paula Puddephatt	138
The Chieftain	Bill Brierley	139
Joined By Rites Of Wisdom	S Grayson	140
Son And Moon	Alex Warner	140
Old World -New World	Angela Helen	141
You	Kelly Cortés	141
Car Boot	Mary Jelbart	142
Over The Top	Katy Holderness	143

SWAN

The hard wet surface of the High Street
Ripples through the running legs of people
Too busy to see the brooding swan
Gliding up the glimmering still river
Which still flows slowly into the shivering sea
Beneath the street beneath the million feet.
They rock and swirl, these roving feet
Like rapid waters among rocks
But the sea is as serene
As only the imaging contemplated in exhaustion
Can be. Could be. Should be.
Was but will not be again
Unless imagination cracks this culverting
And lets the river free to flow again.

A F Brown

NOT TODAY

Beautiful valleys of golden summer green,
Stretch forth beyond the winter that was here.
People ramble around the many peaks,
As I hold you near and hold you dear.

Summer's horizon is purple and gold,
Like the autumn's eye.
Many, many lives that once were broken,
Are mending with a sigh, going by the by.
'So, come on down, down to me'
Cos nothing can compare to this, not today.

Not today.

Simon P Jones

WINTER MEMORIES

The trees have now spread their leaves,
In forest glades, carpeted lawns wait to receive
the coming of the winter snows,
A gift from God in Heaven who knows,
That hedgehogs and voles must hibernate,
To await the spring, when they will awake.

But, meantime, the ground is very cold,
And hills and mountain streams get old,
Skeletons of trees - without their cloaks,
And this mantle awaits, before winter provokes
its white blanket, o'er the countryside,
Makes everything look dead, but has not yet died.

The rabbits' food hidden from view,
And the fox is seen, in the wintry morning dew,
Quietness surrounds this mighty land fall,
And the crispness of the air, richly enthrals
us all, of memories, long ago,
When we were, all children, growing up . . . just so.

J Harper-Smith

RENAISSANCE
(For Jennifer)

I sank slowly into
The Darker deeper,
It was like a quicksand
And slime that closed
My mind until that
Mental property turned
Into itself

Then I met you and
You began to heal
My mental wounds
And you took an
Interest in my untapped
Potential as of some deep
Moving Exploit - I loved you for that

Gerard Allardyce

NIGHT DEMONS

No raging moon this darkest dawn,
The nightmare reel is real indeed.
Stiff arms and fingers ache, a coffin's space.
The light becomes my greatest need.
With black pen and thoughts pulled from my head,
This nightly torture separates sleep from sleep,
Then 'ping' the mind is on another plane
And shoots from dank, deep moat to castle keep.
The scene is lost to a distant haze.
The bladder gnaws and staggers to release.
A church bell tolls the ending of a dream
And the air returns to early morning peace.
My crazy head, like coming off a fairground ride,
Once more the bed envelopes this shambling form.
Demons in my thoughts grow distant soon,
Their deathly grins fade as I'm growing warm.
My ears still sing a one note ring,
Asleep, awake, I care not which or how.
Oooh, sleep's strange memories, how cruel and so soft.
Is this another nightmare or the sleep of angels now?

Jerome Kiel

THE SUNNY HOURS

When I look back upon my childhood years
It seems as though the sun forever shone.
The ripening wheat, the woolly sheep,
Were bathed in golden glow.
Beneath its rays I played and walked,
Exploring lanes and woodlands,
And when the winter months came round
The sun's rays sparkled on the snow,
So deep and fresh and pristine.

And yet -
It must have rained.
I must have felt the wet grass round my feet
And raindrops driven by a cold east wind.
I must have splashed through puddles deep
And sloshed through grey fast-melting snow.
I must have sat before the fire
As rainstorms lashed the windows.

But every time my thoughts return
To country childhood days,
The sun forever seems to shine,
No cloud on the horizon.

Roma Davies

STUBBORN PATH

I'm no joke
Jeer me if you want
Call me a slacker, a no-hoper
Cause I will prove you wrong.
Who is that you'll say
I wish I could be more like him
Look me up, look me down
Cause I'll be who you really want to be

Just because you've taken the steady path;
Just following in the footsteps of many
And I take the stubborn path
I live from day to day while you have your weeks planned out.

The difference is I'm me
But are you who you really want to be?
Try being yourself for a change.

V Topp

SOULMATES
(For Carl; my soulmate and lifelong love)

Is it truly possible to live and breath one being?
To look into their eyes and see as they are seeing,
To know when they are hurting, though you're miles apart,
To hear within yourself, the beating of their heart?

Is it truly possible to be a child and know,
That someone is so special you're never letting go?
To be so distorted with what life has to share,
Yet knowing when he's with you, that no one could compare.

A boy who overcame life's roller coaster ride,
And whilst you travelled yours he never left your side.
A spirit that enriched every time and place,
A humour that enlivened your every childhood space.

He'll never truly know, for I cannot find a way,
To tell him that he is my world and every waking day.
To tell him though we're older, that he still holds my heart,
To tell him when he's absent my world still falls apart.

To show him that I need him, to sleep here by my side,
I cannot speak the words for fear I'll be denied,
Is it truly possible to exist within a state,
Of regret for a love; recognised too late?

Carlamarie Haynes

JAZZ

It's contradictory
Its universe:
Notes, phrases in novel counterpoint
It explores: problems in reverse
The in-logic of its censure
In a bold direction joint
Straddling new and old
Pop and high culture

It takes its stand
Against elitism, its venture
Opting for an influx
A bold adventure
In a studious bid informal
To end racism's crux
Its appeal's private
Yet uniquely global

Individual yet unsexed
Its constant mode
Inconstant, yet discreet
Its seductive goad
Filling a real need
Democracy at its feet
Transcendence a new blend
Is its universal seed

Angus Richmond

THE WATERFALL

I used to like to celebrate
To drink and dance and flirt
Sometimes I would drink so much
That it used to hurt.

Sometimes I would hurt
So then I'd drink some more
One day I left my house
Went out through a different door
It took me to a waterfall
And over the rocks I watched the water pour.

Joe Baird

THE GOOD LIFE?

The willow weeps o'er the water, the clouds weep rain over
                                                    Earth's clay.
The sky at sunset tinged with red, orange, crimson, gold and grey.

The mind is tinged with irony, with doubt and faith, plus known;
The heart is tinged with sadness, pain and joy with love.

The child tingles with excitement. Life, joy, and new adventure;
The parents apprehensive, for protection with the pleasure!

The rose buds into blossom, the girl into a woman,
The lad into a young man, growing into love and wisdom.

That is the great eternal plan! However we get in the way of
Universal Love often times, blocking our path!

Pollution of air, water, lives and childhood dreams.
Damaging hearts with anger and greed, hurting animals and seed.

Withholding care from those in need,
Look only to gratify self, indeed!

Folk die in famines when war rots the land,
Food mountains pile up because bigotry stands.

Generals fight for power and gain, leave their dying people to suffer
                                                    in pain,
Oh, my brothers and sisters! I feel your strain!

Frank Angel

A GYPSY'S LAST GOODBYE

Goodbye my friend we travel'ed far
Forever following St Christer's star,
From darkest Scotland,
To the sunny south west,
Goodbye my caravan, we passed the test,
Our gypsy blood,
I remember it well,
We travel'ed to heaven,
Then into hell,
Through the lost woods of the sky,
You and me, my wife and I,
Goodbye my companion, goodbye my friend,
With you our memories will never end,
And now you must go to another -
Home,
Where my friend,
You will travel alone,
Me I'm past,
The caravan life,
For a house I'll have to strive,
I'll work my fingers to the bone,
And if I can't it's a mobile home . . .

Joyce Healy

SUN RISING

The sun is rising and at its zenith -
the mysterious landscape come to life.
The majestic peaks reach the heavenly blue sky from valleys
full of hope.
And with soft breezes blowing in the spring -
the leaves dance a ballet of free entertainment

Colin Zarhett

THIRD TIME LUCKY

Many of us are too young to remember a war,
but it's not a possibility we wish to explore.
We all know of someone who died in vain,
fighting for their country with no possible gains.

Then on September 11th, a terror began,
terrorists started a revenge attack
Blaming America for their own atrocities
when really it's simply about getting more monopolies.

At first people all wanted revenge,
but now with hindsight many people can see
that all retaliating is doing is giving in to their pleas.
For innocent people are once again dying in vain,
with the terrorists now twisting and shifting the blame.

So leaders of countries please hear our cries,
don't let innocent women and children die,
beaten and raped, and starved of life
limit the numbers of this sacrifice.

Bombing a country may initially stop
terrorists winning the plot,
but for every person that happens to die
a new terrorist is born and grows up to survive.

So the hate and revenge will begin all over again,
until someone learns to refrain.
If we don't there may be no world left to live in,
was it worth it, evil 'Osama bin Laden'?

Catherine Keepin

WHAT IS IT?

Climbing out of the spaceship
The alien grabbed his keys
He'd found the perfect present
For his wife, so hard to please.

'What have you brought me this time?'
She screamed, as she looked in the box.
'It smells hot and nasty
And it's wearing dirty socks!'

'It's only got two arms, one head
And a pair of sweaty feet,
I can't see the remote control
I hope you've kept the receipt.'

'It's sure to cry when it's little
All day, and half the night
Then stay out 'til dawn when it's older
Don't tell me that that's a delight.'

'How do you think I should cook it?
Should I wash it first, d'you suppose?
But what's that runny green stuff
Pouring out of its nose?'

'Could we try to eat it
Except the fluff behind the ears?
It looks as if it's melting,
Must have been there for years!'

'Please tell me what you've brought me?'
Her alien husband smiled:
'I've just found the instructions, dear
Your present is . . . a child!'

Carole A Smith

RENEWAL

Sometimes when the road is bare,
Endless, featureless, without direction,
When it winds uphill over
jagged rocks and sharp crevices,
And the weight on my back,
Makes my legs sag and my feet burn.
Then I know I must stop awhile,
Put down the baggage,
Lie down just where I am,
Close my eyes and for a while sense
Nothing.

Then out of the nothing
Comes a gentle light,
A breeze of peace,
And crystal rain,
Which fills the empty places.
And out of the rocks and crevices,
Tiny seedlings emerge,
Quivering in the breeze.
Letting the rain roll down their leaves.

Growing around me and over me,
Providing shelter.
Scented flowers blossom and
Produce sweet fruit,
I eat my fill.
And strengthened,
Leave my baggage swathed in flowers.
Continue on my way
Still uphill.
But I walk renewed.

N Lord

MISERY

Misery loves company
So I'm going to stay awhile,
I want to embrace self pity
And go that extra mile.

I want to wallow in sadness,
Shut out the world of light,
Give away my heart and soul
Because love's a painful blight.

They say time can heal everything
But I don't want it to heal me,
I'm free to choose what I do
And I choose misery.

A Barrett

WAITING

Why I'm always early
And I'm never late
Cannot keep folk waiting
Shame would be too great.

Something deep within me
Like a hidden clock
Drives me quickly onward
At a fast tick-tock.

When I get to heaven
At the pearly gate
Will they keep me waiting
As they seal my fate?

Robert Dell

THE VALLEY OF THE SHADOW

I passed by the valley of the shadow of Death
And faltered awhile in the shade.
There were many poor sufferers holding their breath,
Casting dice as their fate they assayed.
I sank at the table; my heart was brimful.
The shadows all exits crammed.
I looked in the face of a great, scowling skull
And hearkened the shrieks of the damned.
The gamblers gathered around at the play
Lost slowly, one by one.
Some were borne howling and shrieking away;
Some sank like the setting sun.
The figure of Death, with its black, spreading wings,
O'er the table hovered still.
Dark grew the board as Death raised his hand
And I shrank from his grasping claw.
The howling grew louder; the shapes of the damned
Dissolved and in awful dread I saw
The dice leave the cup. The shadows dispersed
And wings disturbed the air,
A great shining angel gathered me up.
Two sixes were there.

Flora Hughes

HAVE A DRINK ON ME ROSE

Still I can recall
The beauty of it all
The mural and the carpet
Help you to forget
The mess you're in
The movies with the bad men
Do you see them often?

M Vukasinovic

SERGEANT PEPPER ENDS THE EMPIRE

Ghandi and Suez were wake up calls.
But the end of empire
Was truly brought home
On a sixties Saturday afternoon
When Mick McManus was body-slamming Jackie Pallo,
And father was moulding bait from stale Mother's Pride.

My brother,
Dandy/anarchist by nature, came home,
Proud as punch, by the front door,
With a shocking red guard's tunic.
Gold epaulettes shimmered.
Brass buttons stood out like ceiling bosses.
Red and blue braiding criss-crossed the breast.

My father, apoplectic, engaged him.
This was the Rourkes Drift,
The rearguard action of a generation.
While he could tell you everything about Napier at Plessey,
Gordon of Khartoum,
He knew nothing of Sergeant Pepper,
Preferred the '1812' to Captain Beefheart.
My attention was half-Nelsoned
Until the garden gate was slammed.

Confectionery soldiers are no match for real ones.
My brother was made to take it back.

Later that afternoon,
He returned
(By the back door)
With yellow tartan hipsters.

P Ardern

WARRIOR

You have been sheltered, not protected.
All your life you have fought
To keep your corner unmolested
Starting a fight in an empty house
Is your main hobby,
Never caring what comes out of your mouth
Putting your foot right in it.

You have been picked up
Then put back down.
You were seen crawling on all fours
Howling through clenched teeth.
Even though it sometimes hurts
Still you refuse to compromise
Like a punk pulling a nasal chain
The cathartic value of suffering.

Trance out, baby, trance out
Let me live in rooms in your eyes,
Do not leave without me, let me feel it to
Give me a key to unlock your secrets
Perform it baby, perform it
Spoken graffiti turns the air blue.
Punk rapper makes a verbal protest.
Being with you is so arresting.

When will this storm
You have raised up blow out?
Let me ride your wave one more time.
Let me be your warrior
Your shield, your guide
Do not leave without me.

Ian Barton

ROUTINES

His name was Thomas Freebee
He lived by the river bank
Got up at six each morning
But the rest of the day was blank

He wanted to be a fisherman
But couldn't catch a fish
Then tried to work as a forester
For that was his father's wish

To cut down a tree or fell it
Needed a great deal of strength
But Thomas was weak and feeble
And only five feet in length

His life was boring and irksome
Every day was exactly the same
'Til he thought of a way to change it
And out of the doldrums he came.

A routine was just what he needed
A regular way of life
To give himself purpose and clarity
Direction and freedom from strife

So when he got up in the morning
He'd run five times round the house
Tickle the trout in the water
And help the cat catch a mouse

He gathered some wood each morning
Until it was half past eight
Then a fire he'd light to warm him
And sit down an hour to wait

For his breakfast at nine thirty
He toasted some bread in the flames
Put water in the kettle
And joined his young friend James

They sat in the warmth for two hours
Sometimes more sometimes less
Then it was time to clear
The crumbs and the usual mess.

A bit of a run in the sunshine
Or a walk round the park in the rain
Then it was time for luncheon
And it started all over again

Food and drink and talking
Washing the dirty crocks
The afternoon was a problem
Solved by darning some socks

And so it went on every morning
Afternoon and night
Young Thomas was getting weary
With depression and lack of delight

So he tried to get free of the tedium
Of routines from morning 'til night
His only friend had deserted
And nothing he did was right

So he got himself together
And bought himself a clock
To live again by formulae
Before his mind ran amok

So once again he rose at dawn
And slumbered in the dark
At least he knew he had control
Now running three times round the park

Audrey Petersen

Tae The Bard - Rabbie

The time flies past - anither year
tae drink a toast, the bard tae cheer
tae listen tae the words o' one
who feels the fear frae those who run
frae moose who panics in his breastie
tae Tam who flees frae ghost an' beastie,
tae revel in the puddin' feast
a muckle haggis, piped - no least
washed doon wi' nectar in the glass
gold in colour, oh! Whit class
that tonsil-ticklin' whisky brew
when yin sees a' wi rosy hue
an' thoughts o' love fair fill yer mind
tae write the words o' heartfelt kind.
The bard himsel' loved all an' sundry
until he wandered hame on Monday
he felt the fear and kent it well
when tae his wife he tried tae tell
'A wisnae oot wi' that fair lass
a wis there masel' in yonder grass
a watched a moose run frae its habitat
och! A man's a man fer a' that.'

Sylvia Gold

SHARING AND CARING

We write each other letters,
With words straight from the heart.
Good news and some bad things,
So much to impart.

Telling all our stories,
That could surely fill a book,
Of life and its accompaniments,
With views so often took.

We sit and write a letter,
Telling how things are with us,
Sharing personal moments,
With those we love and trust.

A letter's so uplifting
And helps to cheer our day,
With news of friends and loved ones,
As we welcome what they say.

We eagerly await our letters
With news both good and bad,
Then when we've read our letter,
Know it's the best thing that we've had.

We read them over and over,
Then put them safely away,
To read and relive the news,
In a quiet moment on another day.

I M Stead

HOW TO TRICK A KNOW-IT-ALL

Don't you just hate it when people know all?
You shout out a question and an answer will call.

One question I promise they'll not have a clue,
Because the answer is only known by you.

So ask them the question, 'What am I dreaming?'
They think they're so clever they won't know you're scheming.

They'll guess about witches with hair of pure green,
And magical unicorns that have never been seen.

They'll guess about mountains of chocolate ice cream,
And bright red steam trains letting off golden steam.

Then they will realise of dreams they know nothing,
And give any answer their brains seem to bring.

Like monkeys, blue bats, green fish, and mad cats,
Pink grapes, shiny toys, cars, planes and hats.

Butterflies, pencils and green kangaroos,
Books, fluffy pillows, white grass and blue shoes.

Paper, dry rain, lunch, breakfast and tea,
They could go on for days like this you can see.

One answer you know that they'll never get,
Because you're dreaming of beating a know-it-all, yet.

Pam Iwantschak

ADVENTURE

A red bird flies over the watershed
Somewhere over the mountains
A green thought of levity
One spring morning

Drift mind ahead
Think of both worlds
Timeless though mutual change
Find peace and truth

Michael Courtney Soper

WORDS FOR REMINDERS

Happy are the ones faultless in their way,
Happy are those observing his reminders;
Teach me your regulations.

For your statutes I shall sow a fondness.
I shall not forget your word.
Uncover my eyes, that I may look,
At the wonderful things out of your law.

Roll off me reproach and contempt,
For I have observed your own reminders.
I concern myself with your regulations.

My soul has been cleaving to the very dust.
Preserve me alive according to your word.
I have declared my own ways, that you may answer me.

My soul has been sleepless from grief.
Remove from me even the false way,
And favour me with your law.

Incline my heart to your reminders,
Look, I have longed for your orders.
And may your loving kindness come to me,
That I may answer the one reproaching me with a word,
For I have trusted in your word.

Viv Lionel Borer

ED-YOU-CAYSHUN

My friends can discuss football,
Pop stars, television and beer.
Don't mention environment,
Or Third World problems. No fear!

No intellect ever challenged,
As they arrived at the school.
'Just remember the facts, boys,
Then you won't look a fool.'

Churn out the same old answers,
To ancient questions, once again.
'Write it down; remember it!'
Was the teacher's only aim.

No thought ever given,
To prepare them for life,
To resist coercion of the media,
Or study child poverty and strife.

Other forms of intelligence
Were beyond their tiny scope.
Creative and divergent thinking,
Saw the teacher struggling to cope.

If you had special needs,
They were out for blood.
Talents of the dyslexic child,
Teachers never understood.

If they discard worn-out routines;
Give tasks that demand real thought;
Kids soon will make them realise,
Just how little they really know.

John Troughton

JUST A GAME

A bevy of talent, in red and blue
Await the signal to do what they do
Wide, light, straw hats deal with the sun
A lady steps lightly, match has begun
An elegant sweep, has a ball sailing down
To stop where the maid would have it be
It's small and white, 'tis moved, put right
On a spot way down on the green
Large black ball is trained to go down
To gently lean on the jack,
That white ball lies alone,
So elegant, so smooth,
Next bowl is delivered
The ball biased to bend,
An invisible force comes from the jack
Slowly guiding, a prayer is heard
The power of the arm has lost its charm
Too short to do any harm
Each pair of hands has skill
The ball's magic is injected
The hands tell it what to do
One bowler noted the ships out at sea
Drake said, 'Bowl on
Just leave them to me.'
Those sailors never knew
The power of bowls, on the brine
If they come again,
We'll play them, you and me
Any time.

H Cotterill

I AND MY DOG

I'm walking on a lovely white beach,
The soft-looking rough sand rubs against my feet.
Just me and my soft puppy black dog,
Just us in the misty white fog

He looks up at me, with his big brown puppy-dog eyes,
I have to give in to him, and give him one of his favourite
                                        doggy treat pies.

I let my little dog off of his red glittery lead,
He jumps up and bounces around,
And looks up at me with glee.

I love the sea, wind and waves,
The soft breeze that rushes through my hair.

Just me, me and my black fluffy dog,
Just us on this lovely white beach.

R B Manning

A LITTLE WHILE

I have only known you such a little while
But already you have captured my very soul.
To never see you again would mean endless days
And nights full of lonely tears
The road ahead would be filled with sadness
And there would be nought but endless years
If anything should take you from me
The path forward would seem too far
Always to be walked alone.

Barbara Crick

PICTURES ON MY MIND

A book is opened, a book of old
All the pages hemmed in pure gold
The stories opened, stories true
Which I have read, to learn of you
The words they passed before my eyes
Not meaning much, I've truly tried
Today I realised, by listening in
How stories blossom from within
Pictures come forth, they are breaking through
The stories unfolded in depth of you
If you find a picture in your mind
Hold it, keep it, don't leave it behind
One day, you will find
A story, hidden, in your mind,
               will erupt so true
An open picture, of the Lord, loving you.

Dawn P Dodd

FAMILY TIES

We are all set for the journey.
What will the road be like?
We cannot tell until we come to it,
Old age.
Memories crowding in,
Love, care and arguments.
Grandad, Aunt Rose and Jim.
All gone. No.
They rest in Peace forever,
Amen.

Hilda Ellis

Us

Friends introduced us
as natural partners,
belonging together,
fulfilling each other,
matching like gloves.

Our meeting I sensed
as destined as dawn's
succeeding the dark.
I felt the joy of Columbus
on sighting land at last.

We began to know
one another, the unfolding
of buds in the warmth
in spring; then suddenly
the garden aflame with color.

But young love starts out
as a fresh wind: overnight
it may change its course.
We drifted apart, not yet
seeing our bounty of luck.

Soon I became
a sailor becalmed, anxious
for the wind's return.
My calls unanswered, I grieved
in a vale that brought no echo.

To exist without love
was barren; like desert sands
devoid of life.
Walking empty streets at night,
cut off from all around me.

Then you called to say
you loved me still. All at once,
life returned to life!
Joy and merriment galore!
Loudly sound the trumpets!

Classic accounts of love
end here, before the trials
that put it to test
and strengthen the survivors -
as they strongly did with us.

Roger Mather

RED WALL

The craggy lines worn with strain
Take the decades away until the earliest remain.
When our innocence felt raw
With imagination and belief,
The world was Manchester
And the red wall, our mate.
If you were Law then I was Best
Scoring at the Stretford end
In our cherry-red vests.
When the summer sweltered
Great drops of sweat glistened,
We huddled in the shade or roasted in the sun
Still we never left our beloved red friend.
Saturday night discussions after the match,
Our chip paper chilled
In commentary delight.
They said we were mad
But we knew we were right
To stay by the side of our beloved red mate.

Paul Willis

BARBED WIRE

Barbed wire, you stand in the field,
You stand between the concrete and the grass,
You stand against me, so that I may pass another way this day.

Barbed wire, your untold stories, old,
Shall never touch my ears, or unfold,
To be told another day, when the lane takes me some other way.

Barbed wire, your coat, it crumbles in the wind,
Your coat of crusty earth, once brand-new, shall fall,
And the rain shall beat your twisted hands till your bones are naked.

Barbed wire, do you remember your birth?
As so soon death may come from cutters,
When such tools did mould and pierce your luminous skin.

Barbed wire, the sheep that may remember
Your steely glance, have to greener pastures yonder passed,
To leave not a trace, but for a lock of wool you hold so dearly
                                                    in your grasp.

Barbed wire, the cattle pen and shredded corn,
The windmill's blades and wooden tower in the wilderness,
The concrete pavement and farmer's plough, your laws they fear
                                                    to transgress.

Barbed wire, your face so stern, you do not flinch,
As regimental medals, the signs 'Keep Out', fall to ruins,
And street vandals twist and cut at your arms. You stand proud still.

Barbed wire, and though in snow and ice you freeze,
And though the sun forms deserts at your feet,
The grass will grow, and the breeze shall come, to give you
                                        shoes and air to breathe.

And though you fall down, and though you weep,
And though you cry, lonely wails, never heard,
Your dying wish, the rising sun, will cover your face as you sleep.

As men cut you down, and your roots are uprooted,
And the grass burns away, and the oxygen falters,
And your hands, crumbled and shattered, grasp the last blades
                                        of grass they ever shall grasp,
And your eyes, clouded by dewdrops, catch the sun's rays for
                                        the very last time, the very last,
The lock of wool, your talisman, now on the pavement,
                                        I hold dearly in my hands.

Barbed wire, the truck comes and takes you,
Cattle pen, the farmer comes and moves you,
The shredded corn and farmer's plough are not needed anymore,
As the windmill's blades cease to work the cogs of the wooden tower.

Brick wall, you stand in the car park,
You stand between the concrete and the cars,
You stand against me, so that I may pass another way this day.

Dawn Marshallsay

GIFT OF A SINGLE ROSE

So sweet the perfume from your laundered folds,
Seeps idly through your pleats.
Fresh droplets of dew enhance your beauty with sprinkles of charm.
You alone need no others; your powerful stem does stand guarded
                                        but alone.
A paradox, so strong and yet so delicate.
Your bloom may blush or glow, shine or whisper.
The gift of a single rose, a token of love, pride, guilt, remembrance
                                        or lament.

Mary Morley

A WISH
*(Inspired by an old Swedish song my mother taught me
when I was a child)*

I know, I know, what I would wish to be,
A little candle in your room;
I would shine, I would shine only,
I would shine just for you;
I would shine, I would shine only,
I would shine just for you.

I know, I know what I would wish to be -
A little bird outside your window;
I would sing, I would sing only,
I would sing just for you;
I would sing, I would sing only,
I would sing just for you.

I know, I know, what I would wish to be -
A little flower in your garden;
I would bloom, I would bloom only,
I would bloom just for you;
I would bloom, I would bloom only,
I would bloom just for you.

Muriel Willa

LOVE FOR A DOG
(1998)

At first you loved me and gave me good food,
Even when I chewed the carpet you were never rude.

Time went by and I became old
I was skin and bones and very bald.

You bought a new pet, a tabby cat,
Who would purr and miaow at you as you sat.

I tried to copy her, we got into a fight,
You locked me outside for the rest of the night.

I got a cold and always shivered,
Every time I saw the cat I quivered.

I went to sleep and never woke up,
The very next day you bought a new pup.

Laura Somerville

AN ALIEN

I am an alien encircling the Earth
Assessing these people to see what they are worth
What I see so far is not very good
Or perhaps it is me that just misunderstood
These Earthlings are ruled by power and greed
Using up resources more than they need.
Some people have much, where others have none,
Where have the land and the animals gone?
The sick are still suffering, that is not meant to be,
For this Earth has all the answers and the remedy.
Why are these people still fighting each other?
Have they not yet realised they are sisters and brothers?
They are all put together in just one place
It is just one title called 'The Human Race'.
Some kill for power and greed
Others kill for the habit they feed.
Others kill for land, they want more
This sort of killing, they call 'war'.
I am an alien encircling the Earth
I have assessed these people and they seem full of hate
I think we will take over before it's too late.

Jean Roberts

CHOSEN

Working in the family shop,
The twins would make me serve,
The man that came into the shop
They called Casey Jones.
He had a lovely motor bike.
He took me for a spin,
And what a lovely man he was.
I blushed at him, and it showed.
He asked to take me out one day,
And the twins made sure I went.
Three weeks later we were engaged.
What a shock for all.
We loved each other very much,
And felt it at just a touch.
He had a house, just for him.
A great three-bedroomed house.
He said 'Will you marry me?'
I said, 'Say that again.'
I knew I loved him very much
And could not part from him.
He put the ring upon my finger,
As gentle as could be.
The wedding was not long to wait.
Everything went well.
I gave up working in the shop,
And had a holiday.

Heather Ann Breadnam

POSTERS

Looking for bumps these past five years
Having smears each week
Means I'm OK and anyway
I'm too deep-voiced to speak

Of such things to these patients
Sat waiting as I am
Present array could cause affray
Seeing I'm the only man

Postered health, remedial bills
Tarnished on the walls
Around my doctor's surgery
The same each time I call

Friends of mine, the learned kind
Whose words grow white with age
New ones come and soon are gone
But some grow wise and sage

Staples, capable of wear
And having new ones take
A corner off, few words obscured
Leading to small mistakes

The bear that likes his veg each day
(I've seen the salient lines)
Caught measles, passive smoking
And the flu jab's made him blind.

Peter Asher

HOW CAN YOU?

How can you describe a meadow, when it is full of wild flowers,
Or the smell of the honeysuckle, as above the ground it towers?
Or the pheasants down the field, you can hear their squawking cry?
How do you describe those mornings, when blue just paints the sky?
How do you describe those mornings not marred by human sound,
Or the mist so gently rising, as it rolls across the ground?
When it is going to be a hot day; you can smell it in the air.
Look at those deer down the field, you have to stop and stare.
How do you describe the clear water in a river,
with the ducks all swimming about?
Or the colour of the weed and the jumping trout?
How do you describe the dragonfly, as it flits in and out the reeds?
Or the air filled with tiny parachutes, they are only seeds.
How do you explain the beauty and mysteries that are in nature's trail?
Such wonders to behold; its surprises never fail.
Don't forget fresh picked blackberries, taken from the wood.
How do you describe it all? As if you ever could.

Ken Mills

MAN'S FOLLY

When we opened our eyes on the day we were born,
Was it realised it was millions to one,
That we would be human with thousands of species to choose?
A responsibility in the future to come.
But alas, man did not think he owed compassion to the rest.
He hunted and killed for the pleasure.
He destroyed the forests, he polluted the seas
And even affected the weather.
But the day is near when he will have fear,
Like other species have done.

A J Lawrence

THE MASTER ARTIST

The Master Artist is at work
Painting the beautiful sky you see
Unlike Leonardo da Vinci and me
He paints by the power of his word
That is the way of the Master Artist

He makes the sky so beautiful
So beautiful yet peaceful
Oh! How I long for that peace
Which flows from glory with much ease
That peace of the Master Artist

The sky can be bright and sunny
Or it can be dark and cloudy
Whichever he chooses it to be
It's always the work
Of the Master Artist.

Funmilayo Ojedokun (12)

ADAM'S RIB

I saw her once
and found the sun
in the long deepness
of the sky pocket
bit into her moon
knew her at last
heard the blues playing
in hidden depths below
her ever-changing sea
where the angels sit and whisper
it is us from the deep
come swim with me.

John Ball

THE SURGERY

Eyes upon me,
When entering this room.
They always do,
When you do,
Julie's on reception,
'Can I help?'
With a smile,
Take a seat,
Sit for a while,
I see faces,
Filled with utter gloom,
Few do but smile,
Twiddle fingers,
Fidgety feet,
Coughing,
Coughing,
Legs keep a'crossing.
Reading read magazines,
Nurse Jane
Shouts someone's name,
Heal the pain,
That's plain.
'He's running late'
A voice says,
'I know,' says another.
Be late now
To meet Mother.
Kevin Jones
For Doctor Gould.
I hear my name
In and in, no time out.
Reception beckons again,

Leah is now seated,
Soft silky sexy legs
Another appointment
One month's time,
Early one,
Leah, that's fine.

Kevin Michael Jones

BUT WHERE DO I GO FROM HERE?

But where do I go from here?

Which bittersweet path now beckons - which leads,
though falteringly, to joy and which to grief,
dressed now as garish fortune?

Or does true fortune walk disguised - as anguish -
to lift discrimination's dark veil
that, for too long, has dimmed our minds
and darkened our horizons - to break
our divisive barriers?

What strange truths have we still to learn,
their light obscured by blind despair, by heavy fogs
of doubt; by pain, keen as the cuts from splintered shards
of ice, like frozen glass; uncertainty,
thick as winter's dusk?

You who sit near the fires of eternal spring, come warm
this frost-numbed mind. Spare a flame of that pure
light to melt the freezing grip of this audacious

darkness -

that I need never ask again, 'But where
do I go from here?'

Christala Rosina

THE MILITARY PARADE

cascades of tickertape
 scattering everywhere
  in an avalanche
of overbearing recognition
 for the nation's heroes,
  returned in glory
 from the distant battlefields;
the uniformed legions acknowledge
  the crowd's raucous cheering;
yet joyful bystanders are ignorant
 of war's secret reality;
the existence of dark deeds
  lying concealed
behind the masks of blank faces;
 they stare ahead
 into an empty space,
  impervious,
as through some mesmerising dream,
 to the coming tsunami
  of shame and guilt.

Bill Drayton

RADIATING

Her love radiating like a warm fire
So cosy when she is near
Her love can ignite such warmth in others
Her love could heat a thousand rooms
No bill will she send
This is free of charge
Asking only to be loved in return
She is a fantastic lesson from which to learn

Daniel White

SHY ONLY WITH YOU!

every time I see you passing
without even speaking
your blue eyes
like the sky in spring
to see you smiling
you get my heart flying
to forget my sorrow
and have a hope for tomorrow
try to tell you something
and don't know what I'm saying
to have a shaking
and get my tongue frozen
if you'll approach to take a seat
and hear my heartbeat
what you did to my heart
never met anyone like you on Earth
drowned in the crowd
I see only you!

Hacene Rahmouni

BY LONG

Has it been so long already?
Long enough to have forgotten your face
That face which I knew for a long time

One moment it's there and by long it's gone
Gone forever like a leaf brushed in the wind
Passed along that string

Of where I remember
What happened through my life
But by long it's gone

Lisha Naomi Binns

My Thoughts Of The World Today

As I lay in my bed and think of the world today,
    to me the wars and massacres are here to stay.
And as I look out of the window and look into the sky,
    there is not a day that goes by where there is fighting
mass murder and plunder, and to me the world is going under.
    Some politicians of the world are always talking to each other,
with summits here, and summits there, and nothing seems
    to even come to bear.
This turmoil in the Middle East, oh how I wish this war to cease.
    The solution of this crisis is there, a compromise is there,
but no one on either side seems to want and care.
    The solution is that the borders before the Seven Days War
be retained and peace at last will be regained.
    I wonder when, and how, this solution will come about,
then the populace in joyous raptures will shout.
    But alas, I cannot see this cancer of greed
will always be here to be.

Peter Antonian

To Freedom

Inside me there is a soul bursting to be free
Every day I wake to see the trees and hear the birds sing
And the sights I see and the sounds I hear
Only serve to remind me that I am not free.
My life is bound up with the thoughts and words
Which say nothing about life and love.
Must I always be a prisoner of fate or may I
Set out on another road after loitering here?
I know I must stop if only to listen to the birds sing,
Yes, perhaps today is my personal day of liberation
Tomorrow I may find love, freedom and join the birds in song.

Sybil Curzon

Can't Think, Won't Think

Another car stolen
A man stabbed or shot
Beer bottles stashed for later
Communication is the answer, so we're told
Nobody wants to communicate
Except with a bomb, bottle or knife.
What's wrong with us?
Are we different to other people
Brainwashed, that's what we are
We can't think for ourselves
We listen to leaders who are
Murderers, rioters, stirrers of hate
And we're so stupid. We listen
We can't think for ourselves.

Anne Boyd

The Music Of Life

Listen to the music
That's all around
In the soft breeze
As it rustles the leaves
And the haunting melody
Of the gurgling stream
Cascading down to rocks below
The larks in the meadow
Out-sing the pipes of Pan
A far sweeter music
Than made by man
So sit, and listen
Let the music unfurl
To the joy, and the sounds
Of a wonderful world.

Kathleen Fox-Watson

THANK YOU, I KNOW

I look into the blue skyline in front of me and I know
Thank you for all you have gone through for me I know
For the times you invested in my health, wealth, well-being and
enjoyment I know
The cutest eyes that reflect a world of innocence if not a world of truth

Support in my times of need
A light in the tunnel of darkness
A bright yellow beacon of happiness
A smile that melts all fear and doubt within my soul

Thank you for being all of these things and more to me,
you are priceless
No words, signs, pictures or music could possibly sum up feelings
of gratitude towards you

You are the definition of a *'True Hero'*.

Lynsey Stopforth

UNTITLED

I dream of you at night;
of your amazing eyes and beautiful skin.
I dream of your smile and your voice,
of your laughter, your sense of life.
I dream that I didn't ruin all of those things.
That I didn't bruise those eyes or that skin,
That I didn't take away your smile or your voice,
That I didn't ruin your laughter or your life.
I'll dream of you.
To awaken I will never allow,
For only in my dreams do you exist now.

Sheri-Lynne Dike-Johns

NO REGRETS

The hearing's not too good,
And the memory's not too bright,
But I've heard all the things that you'll hear
And a whole lot more besides.

The eyes are tired and rheumy,
And the walking stick is white.
But I've seen all the things that you'll see
And a whole lot more besides.

I drove fast cars, I raised a family.
Plumbed the depths and scaled the heights.
I've done all that you kids dream of
And a whole lot more besides.

Olive Portsmouth

LIFE OR DEATH

Worry, worry, fear and dread,
Cancer, has raised its ugly head,
Our lives have changed, our time's not ours,
The Devil's in his ivory tower.

Treatments needed, treatments done,
Living life as best we can,
Will we live, will we die?
God is hopefully on our side.

At the end of the day, not all is lost,
Our lives may end, or it might not,
One thing's for sure, as you may know,
Life goes on, if not your own.

Wayne Cotter

NEW BEGINNINGS

If the world could have a new beginning
I would want it to be like many years ago
The children's playgrounds
Looking clean, tidy and well looked after.

If the world could have a new beginning
I would want it to be like many years ago
The people of the world knowing
What to and not do.

If the world could have a new beginning
I would want it to be like many years ago
There would be no such things as
Cigarettes and drugs.

If the world could have a new beginning
I would want it to be like many years ago
To be able to go outside and play and not get snatched
Or to walk out your homes and leave the door open.

If the world could have a new beginning
I would want all these things to change.

Kayleigh Jones

A BEAUTIFUL MIND

The voices within my head
are driving me insane
they tell me all these evil things,
one claims to be God
the other claims to be the Devil
but maybe neither exist,
some people say
that I have a young and beautiful mind
but all I have is a mind in turmoil.

They give me all these drugs
they say that they will make me better
but all it does is make me sleepy,
maybe it's sleep that I really need
at least then the voices will give me peace,
it's permanent sleep that I want
then these voices will surely die!

Chris T Barber

WERE YOU THERE?

While the bombers droned on overhead, and the ARP
Rescuers looked for families, some were dead
In the wreckage, *were you there?*

People lost their lives, husbands lost their wives
Many firemen died while fighting fires
In the docks, *were you there?*

Did you know the old Rose and Crown
Nothing was left, all bombed out, all down
No one found, *were you there?*

Did you see London burn, and at every turn
See the docks burn, like a river of fire
Were you there?

Was your family ever lost, and to your cost
Bombed out, and homeless, with no food
Sometimes no shoes for your feet, *were you there?*

Yes, Britain was at war, for a second time
As before, otherwise we would be no more

Would you like the *enemy*, knocking at your door
Were you there?

Rosemary Peach

GLASSES

They're square, they're round
They're short and long
They come in different sizes
They're thick and thin
Filled up to the brim
Give people different guises
They come in pairs -
In boxes too
You top them up when empty
You sit them on the bridge of your nose
At parties you'll find plenty!
They stop the glare when the sun shines bright
Some might be taken to bed at night
If you haven't guessed
Then I'll give you a clue
A spectacle these can make of you
And it's crystal-clear and plain to see
That a drink is what you get out of, me!

E Kelly

THE GOLDEN JUBILEE

For fifty years, she's been our Queen,
A monarch of which to be proud,
And in the length of all her reign,
A favourite with the crowd.

She works so hard, come rain or shine,
Each season of the year,
Whatever she's feeling, she gives a smile,
There's no one to compare.

She'd much prefer to be walking her dogs,
Or riding her horse on the moors,
But she has to 'dress up' in the best of 'togs',
And go on those endless tours.

Crowds of us will celebrate,
Her Golden Jubilee,
A much-acclaimed, and special date,
To say *'God Save The Queen.'*

D M Carne

PICTURES IN MY MIND

Words rise like bubbles in my conscience,
To paint pictures in my mind,
Ones which may be so breathtakingly beautiful,
That my tears make me blind.
Just a string of letters; a necklace of words.
A mere flight of fancy, or a stark reality,
To the positive absurd.
Come, show me any scene,
Today, tomorrow, or what might have been.
Then a picture springs forth,
From my thoughts it streams.
From a simple daydream arises such a scene,
A picture show, a tantalising tableau.
Transposed into weighty words,
Until on the page it gleams,
For others there to see.
With levity, a reality or pure fantasy,
Which arose from within the heart of me.

Jonathan Pegg

THE MIRROR OF LIFE

I looked in the mirror,
And what did I see?
A happy little girl
I was just three.

I looked in the mirror
And what saw I then?
A lively young girl
By then I was ten.

I looked in the mirror
At last I'd become
A bright young teenager,
My life was such fun!

We looked in the mirror
My darling and me
Our lives were so happy
So loving and free.

Years roll by so quickly
When true love is the theme
This part of my life
Is locked in a dream.

I look in the mirror
And what see I there?
Just a grey-haired lady
'My darling's not there!'

Doris Shaw

THE SILENT SEDUCER

I resisted at the beginning,
Then my heart began to thaw.
Once I felt you touch my lips,
I desired you all the more.
Used any excuse to hold you
At the start of our affair,
And to face a day without you,
Seemed more than I could bear.
I never thought to question
Or consider how I feel,
Thinking you were attractive,
When you had no sex appeal.
But now I've come to realise,
Leaving you is not the end.
The influence you had on me,
Much more than I pretend.
Now I'll strive for freedom,
For it's no use after death,
By ignoring your temptation,
Whilst I still have the breath.
Sometimes I may feel jealous,
Seeing you in other hands,
Therefore, I will try to stop
Giving in to your demands,
And if I can't reject you,
It will be to my regret,
Never thinking I might die
Just for a cigarette.

Harry M M Walker

LIFE'S PILGRIMAGE

As I journeyed in sun-flecked lanes
And bleak uplands,
I sought your hand.
'But one day,' I said,
'I may fail to find its warmth.'

Unsuspecting, the ground crumbled beneath me,
Rocks and rubble crashed past me.
Sometimes struggling, I held your hand,
Sometimes I tried to stand alone.
Weary to death, I fell forward in darkness,
Into the River of Desolation.
The pitiless waves pounded over my head,
I saw gentle hands outreached,
And sympathetic faces - only a mirage?
I cried for restful death
And found your arms around me
Stronger than death, gentler than a mother's love
Inch by painful inch you pushed me forward.
There was a threatening silence,
The blackbird sang.
I opened my eyes and saw gentle faces,
And the green verge of a new life.

Now as I go forward by still waters,
Or in the dark forests where wolves howl,
I know even as I falter
Your arm is round me to the End and Beyond.

Joyce Allan

11TH SEPTEMBER 2001

The day was 10th September 2001 and life went on.
On the 11th September 2001, life stopped.
On the 10th September 2001, New York was cheerful,
On the 11th it was tearful.
On the 10th September 2001, our heroes were pop stars,
Their cars were large.
On the 10th September 2001, some people were happy, some were sad;
They laughed and played, they were cross and glad.
They greeted their friends, they ignored their enemies.
Their children were sweet, their children were not,
But they laughed and cried and were loved a lot.
The people went about their work, the children about their play.
Life was happy, life was sad, but on the whole life wasn't bad.
We argued about race, sex, colour and creed,
And many people's minds were on greed.
On Tuesday 11th September 2001, we realised who our idols were
                                     as they dug endlessly in the rubble
And nothing was too much trouble.
Our children were not playing anymore,
We could not hug them close enough as they came through the door.
We shed our tears and held hands with our neighbours, no matter
                                          what colour, sex or race,
We thanked God we were alive and there was no hate.
We nursed the injured, the dying and the orphans and buried our dead.
Above all we hoped we had learnt in that short time
Not to take all the good things we are given for granted,
And always to remember the day New York stood still.

Joyce Lawrence

WHEN I AM GONE

When I am gone and scattered to the wind
Forgive I ask for all the times I've sinned.
I was but human and the flesh was frail -
But life's important duties . . . did I fail?

When I am gone and blowing in the breeze
My voice you'll hear in rustle of the trees.
Listen. You'll hear of all the love I had
And know that it was yours . . . and then be glad.

When I am gone to dance with merry stream
The life I led was real and not a dream
Good times I had but sometimes life was sad
Yet all in all I'd say it wasn't bad.

When I am gone as dust motes in the sun,
You'll know there's many things I've left undone.
I loved my God, my children . . . and each day
He gave to me to do with as I may.

When I am gone as dust upon the way,
You must not grieve, let laughter fill your day.
Remember all the good times we did share -
Then in your heart you'll know I am still there.

When I am gone, sprinkled on daisies white
Look to the dawn . . . forget the fears of night
That was the time of day I did reflect
On how to use my life to best effect.

When I am gone, no longer to be sought
Just stop sometimes . . . and spend a passing thought
To what we shared . . . the smiles and every tear
And when your children laugh . . . then I'll be near . . .

Pamela R Dalton

WISH YOU WERE HERE

Whilst on holiday in Liverpool
I was treated like a fool.
Whilst on holiday in Hong Kong
my feet did sweat and started to pong.
Whilst on holiday in Blackpool
the weather turned really cool.
Whilst on holiday in Colwyn Bay
a gale got up and blew our tent away.
Whilst on holiday in Llandudno
we went everywhere there was to go.
Whilst on holiday in Birkenhead
I wished that I was dead.
Whilst on holiday in the South of France
I was lead a merry dance.
Whilst on holiday in sunny Spain
it did nothing but rain.
I have had my fill with holidays
I will not be going on one again!

S Glover

WHAT'S REAL

If you take away the fantasy I'm left with little else.
Reality is not an option.
It's cold and hard and frightening, it leaves me in a mess.
It's something I can do without.
Yet logic tells me otherwise, it says go out and do it.
Don't be afraid, just be yourself.
Take a chance, be positive, it's really not so bad.
Reality is only life.

Rodney Epstein

HATE

Hate is a room with a door
But no key.
No light can come in,
So the hate must grow.

As time goes by,
It feeds on the dark,
Until all you know is hate.

People pass and offer keys,
But hate has made you blind,
So you do not accept.

With each day that passes,
You hate more and more,
Until your existence is at its death.

Then your hate is only a room.
The door has disappeared
And no keys are offered.

You're left in a room
With no means of escape.
You'll die alone,
With only the company of your hate.

Carman

FALLING STAR

Falling Star is cute as can be
She is never sad but always happy
With a coat of golden fur
And adorable hazelnut eyes
She is always full of surprises

She shares her happiness with everyone
And turns my world upside down
Enchanting in every possible way
Truly is she a very special friend

Niresha Umaichelvam (9)

LIFE

In the beginning,
I felt I was trusted.
Now I know the truth
And I am disgusted.
You spat in my face,
Left me in the ditch.
So now I have learnt . . .
That life is a bitch!

So I've come today
To say 'See you around'
'Have a nice life,
Now get out of town!'
'Leave all your family,
Forget about friends'
'But be certain, make sure . . .
You drop dead in the end!'

Now I've said what I want.
So, okay now I'll go
I just thought I'd write
To let you all know . . .
'It's true what they say,
Believe, it's no lie,
That life is a bitch . . .
And then you die!'

Helen Davis

SCENE OF CRIME

There's a leafy geranium in a pot,
It's called a Scarlet Lady;
And two glasses of bloody Merlot,
Brimming like tears on the table;
There's a ruby ring, but it's only a fake;
A plate of half-eaten wedding cake,
A newspaper headline, on a front page,
Expressing fears for the safety . . .
There's a waxy lipstick as red as hell;
And a watch that will never, ever
Tell the time again, or be wound again,
And there's a tortoiseshell mirror
Reflecting a kiss . . .
It's something that the police will miss,
When they are called.

C Karalius

JOY OF LAUGHTER

Laughter sometimes takes us by surprise
Sometimes makes us wise
And clears the air and gets us there
To people's hearts like piercing darts.
A child at play
Can laugh his fears away
Skies can seem more blue
Angels become friends too
We forget the sadness
And replace it with gladness
And our step is lighter
For the joy of laughter.

Joan Hands

THE CAGED BIRD

Dreams rest in the caged bird's bosom
Her particles of breath seizures
Arrest others and distillate the desire for freedom

You could,
You die for claimed causes
Ideology
You also die because . . .

Moth-eaten lonely hearts ignite their own illusion
And the fire of anguish
Singles wingspan into powdery embers

Shush baby, you must sleep now
Tomorrow the wedding song will be sung
And the golden chain strung around your frail neck
May tighten so don't be frightened
To pull the noose from finger to throat

To dust they melted
Her particles of breath seizures
The dotted red . . .
Thrush and phoenix greet
She will sing our song
Better left unwrit . . .

S Zartashia Al-Jalaly

YEAR ROUND

Spring opens buds along bare, brown bough.
Green meadows call. Flowers scent life's path.
Sun is fruiting the burdened branch.
Dreaming the year, I toil again, and weep.

Pettr Manson-Herrod

BROKEN DREAMS

Lost within the hurt of broken dreams,
You are more to me than you can know.
Never were you just another name,
Names, just like the wind, can come and go.
Every day my heart had longed for you,
Every night I shed a new-found tear.
Moonlight dawned each morning on my eyes,
Showing me that you will not be near.
Words cannot describe the pain I know,
Every time you look into my eyes.
How I wish you knew the way I feel,
How I wish you knew how I have cried.
When I wonder where you are sometimes,
You may be in someone else's arms,
Just like I had longed to hold you near,
Far away from heartache's pains and harms.
But all I can do is watch you here,
In the hope that someday you will see
All the things I feel for you, and that
Even you could feel this way for me.

David Russell

THE SKYLARK

The fields of corn were golden
As we were standing there
We listened to the skylark
Somewhere up in the air

A score of rooks up in a tree
Could not shut out the sound
Of that lovely little skylark
As it came down to the ground

The rooks, the gulls and doves and crows
All making such a noise
Could not drown out that skylark sound
That everyone enjoys

The tractor and the thresher
That cacophony of sound
Still failed to scare that darling bird
The skylark on the ground.

J B Vanson

MUM - A LITTLE WORD WITH A HUGE MEANING

As a little child in the night
Awake with pain or fright
The first name you call is Mum,
When hurt or cut or frightened so much
The first name you call is Mum,
When happy or sad or when feeling bad
The cuddles from Mum never stop.
Throughout teenage years as our angel grows
Our Mum . . . well she just seems to know.
To understand our adolescence
When nothing else seems to make . . . sense
Our mum, she just seems to know.
And as we grow up and fly the nest
It is Mum who knows best,
We learn as we grow and the feelings we show
Get stronger and stronger by the day.
When grandchildren arrive to join the hive
The first number you call is Mum,
So that little word, so often taken for granted
Gets given this massive task
That little word that gives us fun,
That little word is simply, *Mum.*

S G Williams

TO ASCOT

Off to Ascot they did go, all dressed up from head to toe,
Different colours, favourite styles, money for gambling,
                                            wide the smiles.
Chattering in a friendly bunch, in luxury coach to have their lunch
The best the caterers can provide, on to Ascot they eat and ride.
Nibbling bits and bites of that, champagne, strawberries,
                                            'Mind my hat!'
Mindful of the crumbs that mess the perfect clothes in which they dress.
They have arrived, the coach is parked, their beautiful outfits
                                            all unmarked.
Ascot races are renowned, the ladies parade around the ground.
Saw the toffs, heard tipsters' pun, old men with bimbos
                                            blonde and dumb,
Royals in their horse and cart, with their guests looking smart,
Pomp and music from the band, elegant people crowd the stand
A multitude of motley folk, the rich so rich, the others broke.
They cheer and shout until it hurts, then realise they've lost their shirts.
This is what makes the racing way of Ascot and its Ladies' Day.
Hats of all description and size, to wear them, were they foolish
                                            or wise?
Some pretty, some cheap, expensive and nice, men ogle the best,
                                            not once but twice,
Beautiful horses, their form the best, excellent breeding to top the rest,
Foreign owners won some of the races, not all were pleased,
                                            just look at their faces.
Famous people were seen in the stand, a private occasion,
                                            no wave of the hand,
Watched the races, the horses just flew, sang with the band
                                            with a hundred or two.
There was no news of a fortune won, a lovely day out and it was fun,
Hobbling now with feet that are sore, find the coach and
                                            home once more
Until next year, the word goes round, Ascot again, more money found
To have some fun and follow the trends, a ritual with a group of friends.

P Evans

LEAVE ME BE

You don't know about me - you don't know why I am fat
Abused as I was as a child - now how do you live with that?

With your taunts and your jeers - delivered over the years
You neither see or understand my river of tears

This dreadful crime - that is mine
Of not being slim - thus seeing me as stupid and grim
And being unable to do well - because people think I might smell

Unconsidered for jobs - as well you know
Because of being judged as lazy and slow

But let me tell you - you inconsiderate lot
There is a great deal about me that you have not got
Kindness, compassion and the insight to see
You are no better a person than to be able to judge me

The intelligence, talents and wit that I possess
You would not even begin to guess
And you would never find out because you can only see
The outer shell of what makes me

I do not judge you for being thin and shapely
So does this a better person make me?

To walk through life shoulder to shoulder
Surely this is what we should aim for?
No one person is better than another
Only 'different' - which one day I hope you will discover

Unwrap those outer shells and what do we see?
We are all created the same internally
And that makes us even - you and I
So next time you are tempted to taunt me - please just pass me by

Lorna Marlow

THE DECEIVER

Time is like the flutter of a butterfly's wings
when emerging from its chrysalis prison.
Slowly growing in energy and seemingly unhurried
but it's a deceiver, hovering effortlessly,
seeking direction in the blushing promise of a bright new dawn.
Its first flight is vibrant and joyous
but occasionally it pauses, renewing its strength
from the fitful rays of a fleeting sun.
Then, ever restless, it flies forever onward
for time passes like a lightning flash
and with its passing, the glorious wings fade with age.
They are no longer things of delicate beauty,
becoming dry and brittle in the darkening shadows.
Crumbling away, they take on skeletal forms
and swept ever higher on the wings of the evening breeze,
soar away into the timelessness of oblivion.

Paddy Jupp

LOVE ON THE ROCKS - WITH A TWIST

Love on the rocks,
A cocktail recipe.

Take love, well-chilled,
A dash or three of jealousy,
A measure of hostility.
Add plenty of crushed hope.
Stir well. Serve on ice,
Garnished with a twist of spite.

Serves two.
Savour slowly every night.

Brenda Conn

A MOTHER'S WORK

I am but one, with many roles to play and motherhood
                                        is my centre stage.
I must speak with authority and then great tenderness.
I must be firm and hard, and yet gentle.
I must lay down the law and watch it broken.
I must give out punishment and then comfort.
I must demand silence and then become the listener.
I must reprimand bad behaviour and reward good.
I must be a fanatical supporter and there are times
                                        I will let the side down.
I must mop up the tears and replace them with smiles and laughter.
In my moments of weakness I must appear a tower of strength.
I must sometimes take on board great pain, when there is
                                        no longer any room for it.
At the end of the day my task is still not done, for I am only one,
                                        and motherhood is my centre stage.

Robertine Muriel

WHY?

Why is life the way it is?
Many people always crying
Friends and family, some are dying.
Hearts and souls in disarray
The world is changing day by day
The sun may shine to brighten up the days
But why does life fill me with disgrace?
When good things happen, we are so pleased
But none of it lasts eternally.
Why can't things stay good for long?
Why is life the way it is?

Lynda Hopkinson

WEDDING SONG

I want to wake up with you
Glimpse the first rays of the sun with you
Be with you in body and soul
Beyond emotions where only love dares to go

You may have my heart, but take care of it
Its rhythms of life like a play, a sonnet
It's not like iron or steel
Nor mechanisms that do not beat
That do not feel

But of beauty and unimaginable worth
While in your presence should grow and flourish
Like a seed in the earth

Cared for by sunlight, nurtured by rain
Not over protected, drown or scorched by flame
Instead loved, returning to you in the
Freedom you give
To love you and protect you in this life
Together to live

Oliver R Howells

THE LADY THAT DANCES
(For Nancy, a lady I met)

Tall and slim, a little frail
A lovely smile upon her face
When you hold her hands
She dances down the path

Her eyes light up with just a smile
A kind word is all it takes
As she dances down the path
Her balance she can find

Her son is strong, he has her smile
They are the perfect mother and son
I love to see that lady fair
As she dances down the path

This lady is so beautiful
Delicate as a flower
Glad am I that I have met
The lady, that dances down the path.

Carole A Cleverdon

PIANO AND SUNSETS

Music and colour,
My passion, my dream,
Fainter and duller.
Paint the keys,
Play the sky,
Wonder why?
Should be glad,
But music so sad.
Joy has gone,
Drifted away on the wings of a song.
Just piano,
Pianissimo,
Unfinished melody.
C for D, D for E.
As fingers slip,
No sunkissed lips.
No portrait.
Fate,
Said no.
Sad piano,
My echo,
Always.

Carol Ann Darling

BITTER LEMON

The lemon sits atop the chilled liquid
At once looking just as,
At the same time, utterly ridiculous.
I am lemonade - what need I of lemon?

Staring at the beads of perspiration
Dribbling down the slender cut of the glass;
'Did I hear that right?'
Or is the glass gently weeping in sympathy?
Replacing the tears I cannot with
Those subtle tracks that no less carve up the pain.

Why do I mimic the ice
That jostles with the ludicrous slice?
'Just be cool' as the mantra chants,
Blissfully dismissive of the screaming wants.

The eyes betray what the lips murmur,
Feeding the starving captive
Only making him sick
Sicker, sickest of all.
Convicted without ever being at the scene of the crime.
All the time knowing that to starve is to live.
And yet, that one crumb draws you back
Again and again and again . . .

I'm so glad I make you happy
'Another drink, barman, please
No. No ice or lemon this time
I'll have it straight
Just for once - if I can?'

Ah.

I thought not.

'Still, no harm in asking is there?'

Oh.

Sorry.

Alex Swift

THE BEAUTY OF WILLEN LAKE

On thy face I cast my eyes
And drink thy beauty through my soul
Were I like thee but half as wise
I would not be as half, but whole

Each morn I seek to view thy mood
Whate'er that be I'm oft amazed
For if thy beauty were but food
I'd be content for endless days

A hundred times I've seen thy face
In anger and tranquillity
Yet wildest mood portrays still grace
Effecting my humility

So clear the still reflections bide
As painted by a godly hand
Until the movements of the tide
Urge the ripples to the land

And yet in mist of early morn
Beneath a mantle ethereal
Thou soon awaken through the dawn
Thy sparkle makes thy waters real

Christine Barrow

GREN

I remember,
Grooming his glossy coat until every autumn colour
Caught the streaming sunlight,
His reassuring warm breath down my neck,
His liquid eyes brimming with love,
His eager ears readily pointed forward, eager to go.
I remember,
Hugging him as I said I loved him,
Patting his neck as we won!
The only ones in the group to get through the weaves,
Adding treats to his feed.
I remember,
Visiting him in his confined stable,
Helplessly watching his condition deteriorate,
The metallic thud of the vet's boots across the yard.
I remember,
The JCB's entering the field,
Massacring the earth,
Digging an early grave.
I remember,
Squashed together in the clammy stable,
Feeding him treats,
Minutes before he'd die,
Tears threatening to fall,
Stabbing our eyes until they did.
I remember,
Sitting, prisoners, locked away,
Like we were too young,
Like we wouldn't understand,
Watching the clock's hands stumble round,
The radio yelling songs,
Oblivious to what was to happen.

I remember,
The sound of the shot,
The silent aftermath,
The unmarked grave.

Abbie Durrant

IT'S A WONDERFUL THING

It's toast with marmalade,
It's jam for tea,
It's turns to sit on Grandad's knee!
It's summer days, lilac shades,
Tea for two.
It's swinging together, me and you.
It's smoke from an engine,
It's seaside and treats,
It's ice cream and sandhills,
It's old railway seats.
It's old church bells,
Cows in a field.
It's going for walks
How good you feel,
It's happy days, sad days,
It's full of fun days,
It's rain running down window panes.
It's the first *Jack Frost,*
It's a pussy cat lost.
It's oh, so many things,
It gives that something,
Makes your heart sing.
When you feel that life,
It's a wonderful thing.

Dorothy Marshall Bowen

THE ONE AND ONLY SOURCE

You guide me along this long hard life,
And point me in the right direction.
You give good advice whenever I'm needy,
You give me all my desired protection.
A home for me isn't just a house,
Nor a building made of stone.
Ever since you brought me into this world,
I've never been alone.
Mothers are there to care for their child,
Which you do like nobody else.
You have that special something,
Which you do so very well.
Every time I'm about to do wrong,
I hear a voice in my head calling.
It is you giving words of wisdom,
And giving me a precious warning.
You were and are always there for me,
You fill any holes of doubt.
Without money you bring me happiness,
You tell me what life's all about.
I don't think that I have ever said,
How much I love and care.
But I can't describe my feelings,
Because the words just are not there.
You never let me put myself down,
You let me know nothing is below me.
Nothing and no one is above you,
Mum, you are the one and only.

Zoë L Mitchell

WENDY

My friend Wendy
Had to be trendy,
Though growing old
Her heart was cold.
She didn't dare
Get really near
The heart of life
And be a wife.
If it was 'in'
'Twould be a sin
To take a fall
Not have it all.
She thought nothing finer
Than the word 'designer'
And refused to drop
Till she'd haunted each shop.

She didn't know why
She wanted to cry
And thought she'd drown
In her empty surround.
Matching handbag and shoes
Simply gave her the blues
At the very word *fashion*
She flew into a passion.

And then she met Pete
Who slept on the street
And as their eyes met
It was game, match and set.
And for Wendy and Pete
Life became sweet!

Gloria Thorne

SATURDAY

Another wet day
It must be Saturday
Just when we wanted to go
To the beach, the seashore
Oh dear, what a bore
Now to stay home and play on the floor.

The buckets and spades are already packed
Waiting by the door
For the sun to pop through
The sky to turn blue
After this long downpour.

Will it soon pass I wonder
Now one clap of thunder
With lightning to light up the sky
Not a day for a swim
We may well begin
To be glad to stay home, you and I.

Sylvia Bareham

VIOLENCE AND CRIME

The sound of violence is in our land
There's a cry for help, listen to the beat of sound.
We blame ourselves we put the blame on others,
There is a cry for help in our land.

Never were these like this before,
Our town and villages, cities are in ruin.
The problem seem almost frightfully serene,
As the trouble and violence go hand in hand.

The sound of violence is getting louder,
Peace and love seemingly a distant dream.
Pain and anguish, fear and sadness
Is sweeping across our land.

Una Chandler

ALIENS AMONG US

We gaze up into outer space
And ask if aliens exist.
Maybe they're closer than we think;
Somewhere we might have missed,
A little nearer at hand than a distant galaxy.
Could there be intelligent life
In the world beneath the sea?

Have you ever paused to wonder
What a dolphin might think of you?
They are not stupid creatures,
Try to see their point of view.
We are the invaders in their element,
Strange voyagers in ships from alien land.
They see us bring pollution and harm to their world.
If only we would try to understand.

They are kind, gentle creatures living peacefully.
Why can't mankind behave the way they do?
We claim to be intelligent, yet we will create war.
Maybe we should learn a thing or two.
If we are ever visited by beings from outer space
Let's hope that they will treat us with more care
Than we show other creatures when we invade their world
As aliens in this world which we all share.

Pamela Evans

MY INNER CHILD

I went on a journey, to find my inner child.
When I chanced upon her, she looked at me and smiled.
She didn't need to say a word; I knew just what she felt.
I could feel deep down inside me, the things with which she'd dealt.

We walked together hand in hand, and she looked up at me,
Her eyes had filled with sadness, so I sat her on my knee.
I asked her what was wrong; she said she felt I didn't care.
These words ripped into my heart, so my feelings I laid bare.

I told her that I loved her, I was sorry for all I'd done.
I said I'd take good care of her, and together we'd have fun.
I looked into her eyes and knew I'd failed her until now.
I'd try and make it up to her - that's if she would allow.

I'd made her grow up far too fast; a child she could not be.
I'd expected far too much from her and criticised her constantly.
She had to be the parent, the one to take control.
I never should have let her assume that adult role.

She became grown up too early; too early for her years.
Yet no one else was there for her, to dispel her childhood fears.
Her parents - through no fault of theirs, relied on her completely.
I never let her say 'N.O.' - just made her smile sweetly.

Why did I not stand up for her? Why did I not complain?
I guess deep down inside I knew it would be all in vain.
For no one ever listened to the little girl within me,
But now I have decided that, that little girl was sin-free.

I'm going to take good care of her, the little child inside me.
I'll show her what she means to me, and ask that she will guide me.
I trust we'll work together to establish where we stand.
And then we can continue, together hand in hand.

Tina Reeks

RENDER WELL

The early morn, crying, call of the bird
As he waits for the dawn to appear
And with it, the morning,
The lights of on high,
Are clear through
The ever blue sky
Who wakes the minstrel alone in his song
Bright blue as ever before,
The song's in the beauty,
Those notes often cheer,
It seems but no time
Since the nightlife was here,
And birds, to their nests, oft go
To rehearse, maybe song
For the bright, early morn
That cries out in ever on-flow,
Love there to hear, of whatever appear,
The bright notes
Do herald the dawn
Of beauty surrounding its wearily way,
Enhanced with the dewdrops
That come there upon,
How lovely more sound
Of the birds in their song.

Hugh Campbell

ALL IS WELL

The whistling of sad trees
The chirping of famished nestlings
And the cry of a sorrowful people
All can be heard but from a distance

A dog whimpers from afar
Joyful, vicious vultures cluster in the sky
With eagerness and anxiety they wait on the sly
Hoping for what is promising to be

A ravenous child grapples tight
A mother's skirt
Expecting a miraculous morsel to fall
But the plate is full of nothing
For starvation has taken over the throne

The sun is scorching horridly
The grass has shrivelled and withered
They wear a drooping face upon them
The land has remained futile
It has become barren and scornful

Siblings cry for porridge
Yet the pot is full of nothing
Children have become pregnant
Mothers a prey of grievance
Death hovers above
Like a hungry lion, it watches from a distance

Fathers ooze of shame
For they have nothing to give
No rains, no food, no life
The skies have stayed stubborn
The land has frowned on its people

The land of yesterday
A day of honey
All has been but wiped out
The land of today
Nothing but suffering and hunger
Tomorrow will bring nought but more cries
Who will but save them
For all is well not
In the land of used to be

Roseline T Chirape

YOUR SECRET'S SAFE

'Your secret is safe
with me,' they all declare, but
everyone has to
tell at least one person,
who 'doesn't count'.
Might as well have
done and telephone
'News of the World'
direct.
Saves time. Good
news does spread too,
but not so
fast, so far
and wide. Your
secret, once shared,
is safe, perhaps, probably,
possibly . . . odds
vary, of course. It
is safe like internet
banking, or eating beef, or
nearly always
using contraception.

Paula Puddephatt

DOVECOTE

Three white doves
Flew in one day
From over the hills and far away
They stayed with me
For one long year
Became my friends
Had heard my prayer.
'A gift from God'
Is what they were
To keep me company
Through the year
They cooed and picked
The corn and seed
To satisfy their hungry needs.
A gift from God?
Oh yes, indeed!
Then left to seek another in need.
Where did they go?
Back to God?
I'll never know
For they only stayed a little while
Perhaps they came to make me smile.

Lyn Peacock-Sayers

REQUESCANT IN PACE

The clock is chiming, chiming
The knock is at the door
The light is getting dimmer
Soon you'll be no more.
The conscious now unconscious,
The flickering eyes now close,
The Lord be with you dearest
As you lie there in repose.

I know you are still with me,
I feel your spirit here,
With the maker of all makers
You've nothing left to fear.
Your face will never leave me
Your love still fills my heart,
Although I cannot hear your voice
We'll never ever part.

Carmel Lynch

MADNESS SQUARED

If I could
I would
Would what?
You know what
No I don't
Yes you do
No I don't
Tell me
You know
Please tell me
Okay

Well if I
Yes, yes, go on
If I could
What
I would
Tell me
Cure my schizophrenia
Oh!

Paul Stevenson

ROUND THE WORLD

I'm going round the world, with my little girl.
We had to go, look at the time,
It is already half past nine.
We went in the hot air balloon, up in the sky and over the moon.
Tick-tock, tick-tock, already 1 o'clock.
There we were, going over the sea, already time to take our tea.
Then I had to go to bed, with a really sleepy head.
The next day when I woke up, I had a drink in my favourite cup.
Then it was time to have our lunch,
I started to shout, she gave me a punch.
I nearly fell over, what will I do? I do not know, how about you?

Sylvester Espana

BIG NOW

This love swings in the Big Now
a comet zoom zoom zooming
across the universe
all starlit and sparkling
all soaring and spinning -

all caressing and curves and contours
gazing in wonder at beauty and
lying bathed in dawnlight
with birdsong and gentle rain-falling
your breath slow-wind and tendersoft
a whispering before there was time
a place of essence
a place of love and weeping
of holding and clasping
to laugh to smile to kiss
to taste to touch to savour
this love in the Big Now . . .

Alex Dickie

A DRAFT OF SHADOWS

As you sit in your room
Waiting and listening to the rain
Feel the ghosts of poets
All around you
Some famous, others not so famous
But they are all there
Still weaving their patterns of words

Betjeman is slandering Salford
Instead of Slough
Wordsworth's host of daffodils
Has been replaced by bluebells

Robert Frost is no longer
Stopping by woods on a snowy evening
But running across fields on a spring morning
Still with miles to go before he sleeps

Kipling's boy is now a man
And giving advice to his son
Thomas rages on against the dying light
Truly in keeping with today's 'fad' rages

So while you sit writing
And waiting for the rain to stop
Draw inspiration from the ghosts
All around you
And perhaps they'll make you famous
Like they all were
Weavers of wondrous words.

Joe Loxton

CEREBRAL CELEBRATION

Behind the eyelids is a screen
Where the mind's design is seen.
A synapse snaps
A pulse explodes in light
The cortex is ablaze with fireworks
Light and darkness, Catherine wheels
And spangles all cascade beyond
The reach of sight. If we could
Penetrate, without a surgeon's knife
And blaze a laser to the source
Of life, then someday, someone
Might perhaps explain the secrets
Hidden in the brain.

Beyond that, is it possible to find
The key, the secrets
Of the mind? The screen is blank,
Poetry is gone and we must settle
For the image of a song.
Poor man - alone in this vast
Universe - can only contemplate
(For better or for worse) wherein
The darkness is the spell which
One day, may, proclaim us 'well'.

Behind the eyelids wise men's
Eyes can see, perpetually,
They see the light there in the dark
Which proceeds the early morning
Lark and while we thrash about
Uncaring, we can cling to this -
That light to life is like a tender kiss.
Unknowing -
No one needs despair
For long when he can listen
To another's song.

A synapse snaps, a rocket in the sky,
The northern lights ignite
The dark cerebellums glow
And stars fall just like snow.
Within the cranium small tapes
Of memory in *DNA* display
The imprint of a distant,
Half-forgotten day.
Great shadows dance where loved-ones
Re-emerge and prance against the passage
Of the night. On silent tiptoe
Sunbeams gather.
A full-blown dream emerges - Rupert
Runs across a carpet on a cloud
And all the leprechauns of Ireland
Shout out loud though nothing stirs.

A synapse snaps and all these
Images collapse. A synapse snaps
Without a whimper,
Or a scream and we surrender
In a dream.

Michael Bell

FRUSTRATION

These shoes, so beautiful, so delicate,
Make one walk blissfully tall.
Spreading elegance, enhancing gait.
No good, folk say, much too small.
Settle for the usual wide 'flatties' I hate.
I'm told my visions of youth are wild,
Sheer flights of fancy, as from a child.
Nowadays I am pressured to do as others think I ought.
Me! Approaching old age? Perish the thought.

Olive L Groom

PLOUGHING A FURROW IN THE FIELDS OF MISERY

Pestilence and death, the main charges,
Assisted ably by war and famine
Ploughing a furrow in the fields of humanity

The Reaper at the helm,
Cherishing the abundant harvest.

A black swarm, their seeds of evil
Scattered nonchalantly,
Its potency recognised.
That first crop, flowering further the fields of misery.

Ignorance, confusion, guilt and self-pity
The soils upon which the crop would fester.
Black fruits swollen upon scarlet stems,
The agony of the harvest.
The diet of the Reaper, feasting upon his handiwork.

War and famine, the main charges,
Assisted ably by death and pestilence
Ploughing a furrow in the fields of humanity . . .

James Gibbons

LAST NIGHT

Last night
You loved me truly,
You held your hand in mine.
Why can't it be like this
All the time?

Last night
I cried on your shoulder,
To wipe the tears away
Why can't it be like this
Every day?

This morning
As we parted;
Your face
Was full of pain.
Why can't it be last night
Again?

E J James

FOOD FOR THOUGHT

Children are dying
I've got tears in my eyes
Their bodies are bloated
And covered in flies
They look at you
Their eyes full of hope
But their mothers cry
Because they can't cope
Why in this world
Of trouble and strife
Do all these children
Give of their life
Seed, food and water
They need to live
Governments and people
The world over can give
Think of these children
And their urgent need
Supply them with water
Fresh food and seed
Look at their eyes
Give them some hope
And hope for their mothers
Who cannot cope

Ivor Emlyn Percival

A DAY AT THE ZOO

We had a day at the zoo
There was many animals to see
Some of them pulled funny faces
Others just laughed at me

We saw the stripy zebras
One with a baby at foot
He galloped around with his tail in the air
And drove his mum off her nut

Then there were the elephants
With their long trunks, spraying the air
Walking up and down their enclosure
For the people they just didn't care

And then we came to the monkeys
They really made me laugh
Throwing all their fruit and veg
At the unsuspecting staff

Then there were the giraffes
With necks that reached the sky
If I ever wanted to talk with them
I'd have to grow ten foot high

Then I saw the lions
They were lying in the grass
The cubs were all frolicking around
And the little one bit its mum on the ass

We came across the camels
Some had one hump, others two
They didn't like the public
They spat and it went on my shoe

Then we heard the bears
So off I went to see
There was this big brown bear
Climbing up a gigantic tree

Then it was time to leave
We had to go home for tea
I thought about those animals
Thank God it wasn't me

Julie Hampson

THE QUIET TREE

Suddenly the tree has changed into a new pale green
Singing out in its own way that spring is here again
It's like a little miracle where all the buds come from
On that old tree which stands out there, neglected and alone
In summer he is fully dressed and every bough is laden
With rich and healthy bright green leaves which will create a haven
For birds cannot be spotted as they rear their babies there
And the squirrels play for hours, climbing in it here and there
Then slowly that bright green will fade, and make way for the autumn
These colours are quite magical, it's like a fairy paints them
Russet - yellow - orange - brown, with some around its feet
The old tree looks so beautiful when summer is complete
And for a while it stands so proud and looks like burnished gold
How does anything so lovely come from something quite so old
But have you ever looked at it against a dark blue sky
Just as the day is ending, but it isn't really night?
Each branch and every twig so very clearly can be seen
It's a different kind of beauty from the gold and from the green
So if you enjoy that big old tree and all the pretty colours
Of palest green, a darker green and red and brown and yellows
Please take another look at it as you go rushing by
And you'll see it still looks beautiful against a winter's sky

Dorothy C Blakeman

TODAY I WILL!

I will not shout, I will do that,
Tomorrow!
Today! I will laugh,
Tomorrow,
I will cry,
Today! I will be nice to everyone,
Tomorrow
I will be impolite,
Today! I will smile,
Tomorrow
I will frown
Today! I will,
Smell the flowers, look at the sky,
Watch the birds in flight
Paddle across a stream
Walk through a dappled sun forest.
Sit in the sun, have a drink,
With friends.
Today!
I will watch the ocean waves,
And the sailing ships,
Hold my children tight,
Not say no to my grandchildren,
No matter what,
Be patient with my husband!
Today!
I will walk through a meadow,
Sit and gaze ideally at the playing lambs,
The grazing cows, catch a glimpse
Of a running rabbit.

Today!
I will watch a storm in all its glory,
Laugh when caught in the rain.
Eat all my favourite foods.
Tomorrow I will diet!
Today!
I will smell all the fragrant flowers.
Watch a butterfly in flight,
The bees as they take their pollen.
Tomorrow yes tomorrow,
I think will take care
Of itself
All the todays! are ours
To share with everyone,
And sharing with us
Is God.

Wendy-Elezabeth Smith

MEMORY OF THE QUEEN MOTHER
(Dedicated to the Queen Mother, Royal Ascot 1998)

Attending the course of Royal Ascot,
A moment in time have not forgot;
Corned beef sandwich and coke in hand,
With officer chattering, roadside did stand.
Blue lights encumber a dark limousine,
A cycle escort to guard the Queen;
Queen Mother herself was sat inside,
Quick thinking, I bowed and food did hide.
Not to be rude as past they filed,
As I looked up, Queen Mother, she smiled;
Amusing act or just polite,
Reaction to this comical sight;
That grand old lady, fond memory,
One fleeting glance when she saw me.

Andrew Bray

AN APRIL WEDDING

With the dawn chorus gone,
and the morning light shining
through the swelling buds,
and the day slowly blooming,
and the slight mist lifting,
the activities begin.
The bridegroom - silent - breakfasts
then starts to dress,
tall, elegant, for his bonnie lass.

Across the road controlled turmoil,
comings and goings,
bouquets delivered, last minute guests,
faces appear at windows, looking heavenwards,
will the weather last?

A small crowd gathers,
muted voices, giggling girls,
neighbours peer by garden fences,
groom and friend are quickly whisked away.

The mother of the day comes into view,
smart, cream-costumed, grateful for the fact
that her charge is almost ready.
Cameras click. Smile - that's it!
Pulses quicken, passing nuns
wish all the joy in Heaven.
Quiet gasps of admiration
for laughing bridesmaids
as they too go churchward bound.

And now the lovely, smiling bride,
and at her side her father,
proud as any peacock ever was.
And as their eyes meet
she sees amid his joy
a silent tear.
A pity he could not be here;
the April wedding means his gifts will last.

John Walmsley

MERELY A PLAYER

Glass shatters as I throw
No care for formality
I am *me* now,
So use the glass on my skin
Strike me I feel no pain.
Frightened at my own reflection
As cruelty and carefree possess me now.
Imprisoned in a cold ward
Chinese eyes watch me from afar,
And my mind takes a trip of its own
I don't walk on water anymore, I drown
I don't walk over clouds, I fall from them.
It's just my mind choosing a different subject
and not choosing to pay attention.
My shell suffers and makes me look bad
I am not mute, I speak to myself.
I am the teacher, but I've lost my goal
My mind is but a pupil
And my pupil disciplines me
So I am no teacher, but merely a player
And I lost the game.

Helen Bulford

NEMESIS

Black helmeted, insect bodied
He mounts his metal charger.
Spins gravel, acrid fuel, dust and ashes.
Exquisite noise, off-set by
- Cicada, crickets, night's raucous chorus
He roars off until the end of the night.
Headlights; fireflies, piercing blackness!
Pulses racing - faceted eyes glowing.

Enter car, purring prowling.

- Tortured metal,
- Twisting,
- Scraping
Senses reeling,
all forgotten.

The spinning road reels up
to swat him . . .

S A List

A FREEDOM 'HERO'

To the square returned,
The 'warrior' bold,
To the shouts and the roaring cheers
Within his heart, burned a patriotic fervour.
For the deed he did
Was a deed most foul, which all
But his countrymen jeers
A woman lay in the street, so cold
Killed! By the 'mighty hero'!

Ron Wakely

UNTITLED

It's time to walk the Chinese wall
Take with you best wishes
From us all
The funds are there
They've all been raised
So many events
We're really amazed
The hours of training
So many miles
To help special people
Regain their smiles
You must feel quite proud
That right from the start
A great many people gave
Straight from the heart
So whilst on your great trek
Remember this thought
You have all our love
And our total support

B T Bell

POEM

I think
I recall
eternity.

But I know
that I am
not yet ready
for eternity
to recall me.

June Hill

LISTENING

If sand could tell a story
What a story sand would tell
Ten million words of stones upon the beach
The waves the pages of the book to reach.

Endless time upon the shore
Watching, listening, rolling, glistening,
Each movement governed by the seas
Inhabited by all who dream.

Some short and thin
Some long and fat
Some flat, some round
Like diamonds laid upon the ground.

Some wet, some dry
Blowing winds drift up to the sky
Some white, some brown,
Some black, some blue
The colours in our eyes all new.

Warm sand you move along the beach
Your stories change each day to teach
That life is good for those who reach
For those who hear the wisdom preached.

Oh sands of time help me this day
To stop and stand one moment more
To look and look at my seashore
I understand you more this way
My wisdom comes from when I pray
That God lives in me, every day!

Talbot Tully

LOST VOICES

Children shadowy stand
looking on
silenced by tradition
voiceless

Women too
transfixed
dumb
voiceless
forever
their story untold
in male squashed
power-driven
history

Time locked figures
cry
listen to us
in the sighing wind
listen
in the rustling trees
to us
and
liberate
resurrect
we
who too have lived
Earth's dream.

June Fox

TRANQUILLITY

Listen to the raindrops
Weaving their magic spell
And you will find
They have a tale to tell

The mists unfold
To turn the page
The prelude
To God's own stage

A sunrise
That awakes the dawn
And casts the die
That puts serenity to spawn

A spider in a spin
On a dewy morn'
Creating a masterpiece
Of intrigue

A meadow
A rolling wonderland that calms
And fires the very soul
To stir a hint of Brahms

A secluded stream
Snaking in its run
Playing hide and seek
With the sun

A breeze
That gently blows
The buds away
That sows

A solitary cow
Ruminating
Epitomising
The eternal dream

To hear a yellow-hammer
Sound its mournful call
About the time
That apples fall

Starlight
Stealing our thoughts away
To mesmerise
And not a penny to pay

Patrick Morrissey

A GARDEN FULL OF ROSES

Dusk creeps into the garden,
Enfolding all within its shadow.
The heavy scent of roses fills the air,
Evoking memories now long past.

I reach out to touch your hand,
But sadly, find that you're not there.
My fingers rest on crumpled silk,
Fallen petals of a full-blown rose.

This was our special time and place,
Precious moments filled with dreams.
But now our hopes have disappeared
Faded petals blowing on the wind.

And yet, I know in years to come,
Our special place will still be here.
In this lovely garden full of roses,
Filled with memories of our love.

Florence Hall

RAIN

Wet fingers tapping, tapping
In the weeping August dark of sighs,
Moaning,
Mourning departed day.
Its transient echoes fade away
Groaning
In a misling mist, their drear demise
Shrouded in a cloud of unknowing.
The ghost of the blind dark blowing.

Fat tears thronging, thronging
The dimpled glass in the noonday shower,
Sighing,
Decrying the salt-blurred scene
Tomorrow's gold cannot redeem.
Crying
While soft wings test their puny power
Against the unyielding window pane,
Distorting the face of truth again.

Silver slivers gliding, gliding,
Sliding earthward in April's dawn.
Singing,
Winging on Hope's tuned string
Taut with innocent wondering,
Flinging steel arrows where clouds are born
To pierce the veil where truth stays stark,
Releasing the ghost of the bat-blind dark.

Elizabeth Millington

THE LOSS OF A TRAWLER

The Captain on the bridge has stood and smoked the whole
watch through,
the fogs that thick the bows of his ship are hidden from his view,
he stands with his hand up to his ear trying to hear the bell on the pier,
but the only sound that comes from the fog, is the barking of
a playing dog.

The mate has stood and cast the lead, his hands with the cold have now
turned red,
Somewhere above on the towering cliffs there's a white walled cottage
where he lives,
And there below the rocks do wait to tear the ship's thinning plate.

The engineer works below easing the engines as slow as they'll go
with a glance at a gauge and a squirt of oil the ship pushes home
with his ceaseless toil.

The crew are all forward on lookout ready to give a warning shout,
the fog hangs on them like a dew soaks in their clothes and wets them
through but for this fog they'd have now been by a roaring fire,
their wives they'd seen,
with great steaming mug of tea sitting with children on their knee.

And then with a jolt and a sickening scream, a rush of flame a hiss
of steam,
the ship is broken and torn apart the lights go out and all is dark
with journey's end nearly in sight, not one man did last the night,
The skipper, the mate, the engineer, and the crew who'd been with them
all the year,
will finish their journey on the tide, but in no better company could
I ride.

Ronald Blay

PLAY ME

Your curved body, my straight spine
Play me slow, watch me pine
My bridge connects all racked strings
Fiddle me now, hear me sing

Pluck me gentle, strum me soft
Hear my echo, it'll never be lost
Angels play me, Cupid too
A whole lot of love, a new taboo

Pedal me deeper, hear the grand
A soft tinkling, a harder hand
As the hammers hit those tuneful strings
A never-ending circle, the golden rings

Hit me hard, drum me quick
Beat me fast, a powerful hit
Your added anger, I've lost my tune
An unravelled melody, a broken loom.

Alexa Raisbeck

THE DRUM

What of the drum?
Whose primeval ancestors
Evoked mystical images.

It speaks to the soul
And shouts its commands,
Controlling battles, pulsating.

The drum is dominant,
The drum is social,
Soothing and healing
Through rhythmic repetition,
Reminiscent of a mother's heartbeat.

So what of the drum?
This simple entity
With its awesome power!

Mike Tinsley

LOST CHILD

Little child so meek, so small,
you didn't stand a chance at all.
The odds for you were stacked so high
there was no point for you to try.

The battle lost before it started,
your mum and dad left broken hearted.
To witness first hand the wonders life can hold,
but yours was a story never to be told.

You were never meant to splash in puddles,
ballet dance or wear ribbons in your hair.
Not for you tap shoes or Barbie,
never to know the love of your parents' care.

Precious infant in God's hands
your darkness turned to light.
Cradled in his warmth and glow,
forever a star shining bright.

Grace McGregor

A FRIEND

A friend is someone who smiles with you
And is happy to hear your voice.
Who is there every day
When you need them to say
Everything will be alright.

A friend is someone who is honest with you
Even when the truth can hurt.
Who will dry your tears
And wash away your fears
And be there when you're in despair.

A friend is someone who is there with you
Through times of joy and sorrow.
Who will give you that hug
And will never be smug
When your world comes crashing down.

A friend is someone who shares secrets with you
And who with your life you trust.
Who may be miles away
But is in your heart to stay.
Someone you think of every day.

A friend is someone who laughs with you
Even when stories are dull.
Who shares private jokes,
The person you love the most.
To me that friend is you.

Emma Tagg

I AM BLESSED

I am blessed
For I cannot love
Not for me soft whispers in ears
Or unashamed shows of affection with tears
When you love someone so much
The trembling inside of feelings so intense
Not for me
For I am free
The musty smell of the person you adore
Brings instantaneous flashes bouncing round your mind
Why do you ache inside?
When this person who has invaded your life
Is not beside you
I am blessed
For I am blind
Fools who bare and share their souls
Entwining their lives
Amalgamating goals
Being there for each other in times of pain
I am blessed
For I refrain
From showing my emotions
These poor pathetic fools
They cannot grasp what it is like to be alone

I am cursed
For I cannot love

Gavin Clements

KINGSTON

Oh historic Kingston,
A jewel in Surrey's crown.
People come from far and near
To visit Kingston town.

To see the sights,
To see the Church,
And many other things.
Or see the Coronation Stone
Where crowned were Saxon kings.

There's much to see
And much to do
To fill your heart's desire.
'All Saints' on a Sunday,
The organ and the choir,

On other days to view the bridge,
Or boat upon the Thames -
Delights like these keep us secure
And free from sorrow's stems.

They lift our hearts,
They cheer our souls,
They ease the mind of worry.
Oh jewel so rare, you Kingston,
Stand long, stand proud -
In Surrey.

Kenneth Kirby

KITE-FLYING

Dogs and people on leads
walk these public spaces;
grounded aircraft unsnags itself from
wide tramrails strung across grass -
buffeted around runway,
lets the wind take it.

Unleashed bird of prey
swoops - pulls out of spin -
go fly a kite, whirlybird,
scarlet diamond head,
your royal blue tail streamer
writhing and coiling in knotted gusts;
reins curb recalcitrant child:
strings attached
unravel with another
squiggle of airbrushed light.

Far below
a man, arms braced, conjures
invisible lines of force
from fingers pointed upwards:
as this bucking bronco
of the skies, pawing the air, throws
dismounted rider.

Brian Garfield

MORE THAN WORDS

I love you
what more can I say
this is one of those rare times
when my words don't
adequately display
how I feel inside
but I will try
to let you know, to let my feelings show
how much I love you

Baby with every fibre of
my being, with my heart
with my soul
with those thoughts that I tell you
with those thoughts left untold, I love you

With each breath
I take, with each word I speak
with each sigh, smile, kiss and touch
you make me complete

I love you with who I am
I love you with everything
I might one day be
I love you spiritually, physically
and emotionally

Your voice sends chills up my spine
so sexy, so sweet
I love the way you speak
touching you is like magic
I love the way you feel
my skin on your skin
makes my senses reel.

Darling you and I together
our paths intertwining,
or life forces fusing
reaching higher heights
gaining power, gaining strength
truly learning to love and be loved
in the purest form of the word.

Baby, I love your strength
in a land of so many, fronting
weak men, pseudo-players
who are afraid to ask
their women for what they really want
I'm glad that you are so strong
strong enough to tell
me what you need
to open up to me emotionally
to let me be there for you
as you are there for me.

So honey, I thank
God each day.
I always say a prayer
asking him to
strengthen our commitment
true and through
and I thank him
for answering my prayers
Jamal, I thank him for you.

That's how much
I love you.

Lisa Parris

SANTORINI

Rising out of the sea
Sheer, high volcanic cliffs
Layers of black, yellow, red,
Perched at the top
Clusters of white buildings
Shimmering in the heat.

On the opposite shore
A fertile plain,
Here tomatoes are grown, and
There are beaches of black volcanic sand.

In the South
Evidence of an artistic civilisation,
Long ago lost
In a violent eruption.

At the northernmost tip
A small cafe, overlooking the sea
Catching a welcome breeze,
Soft gentle music, hot sun,
Past, present, sea and sky
Became as one.

Joan Sculpher

RECONCILIATION

This is a fortress door, forbidding,
closed over many years.
I come to it late,
wait, unwilling to knock.

Feeding fears, misgivings, tears,
regretting love broken,
I stare at rusty hinge and lock,
and finally despair.

As I turn away,
intended token words unspoken,
I hear you say,
'Come in -
the door is open.'

Margaret Roach

ONCE I WAS YOUNG

Once I was young as springtime:
Drifting on soft breeze of life,
My young mind cluttered with the
Joys of life, the sounds, sights,
And the smells of the new season
Until my head swam in an ocean
Of pleasure, deep and so fresh!

Once I was young in spirit nothing
Was too hard, hard to tackle then: and what
Of now, there are just the memories
Of, past summers, some good some not
So good; the goals I scored the games
I played loved ones that had passed away
All stay within my memories of springtime.

Oh! How I wish those youthful days
Would return once more to fill my
Frame with forceful pace to my faltering
Steps to feel the blood surge once more
Through my veins, to climb and sit
Amongst the canopy of a towering tree
To look back again to when I was young.

Just once! Just once!

Derek J Morgan

POCKET STONE

A smooth, solid stone
Slides slowly
Through fingers into the pocket.
Comfort
Wriggles warmly
Up the sleeve into my head.

I can go
Whenever
I want
To bounce the stone.
Walking on water
By the lock.
Gathering calm
Before it sinks
To rest in a peace
I must renew
With a brother of his
Sometime soon.

Matthew Goodyear

A COUNTRY LANE

It winds
   and winds again
   and takes no heed of speed.
It does not care
   for race and tear
   because . . .
      tomorrow . . .
   it will still be there
   in Dorset.

Kinsman Clive

DEMENTIA DREAMING

'I don't know what I'm doing'
shouts Mother with dementia.
I don't know what to do for her,
but treat her reverential.

She cared for me through many years
of childhood's joys and ills;
Now surely I can care for her -
she seems to love me still.

Although she thinks there's two of me
(and I an only child),
I'm often 'wearing different hats' -
tired, happy, cross or mild.

She put her life on hold for me
so many times before;
Now mine revolves around her needs,
and they get more and more.

Her tights are on the breakfast tray,
her teeth lost 'neath the bed.
The cat appears to be a dog,
she wishes she were dead.

Mothering Sunday came and went,
and so did Easter, as did Lent.
Church was such a joy to her -
now words of hymns a muddled blur.

Her memories and dreams have gone,
all faded with the night.
I wish we could turn back the clock,
and let her wake to light.

Her life was lived in gentle love -
may she soon rest in God above.

J M Gardener

LONELINESS

It creeps up on you when you least expect it.
You never seem to realise when it's happening.
Loneliness drags you into its own world.
Which you never seem to be able to escape from.

Loneliness traps you in its arms.
Never wanting to let go of you.
Not wanting to be on its own.
Hugging you for comfort and support.

Its world is lonely, dark and possessive.
You think that you're the one trapped in your own world.
When really you're trapped in someone else's.
Trapped in someone else's loneliness.

You want loneliness to comfort you.
But really you're comforting loneliness.
Its only fear is when you depart from its world.
When it's left to support itself.

Adam Russell

WHAT DO WE WANT?

If just one wish
Could change it all
Could you stay happy?
Would you still want more?

Could you be content?
With money to burn
Would you feel perfect?
With a body so firm

Will confidence come?
With beauty, good looks
Would you not feel lonely?
With someone to love

Try to stay happy
With all that you've got
Always remember
There's someone worse off

Chris Buxton

THE BLACKBIRD
(Tragedy at sea)

We said our prayers as the blackbird sang,
And the prayers we said were for those that mourn.
But the blackbird sang
And was not sad.

In a far off sea, there were many drowned,
As we heard the news, the sun shone down,
Nor did it cease to shine
In the blackest time.

Though days are bleak
And the mirror dark in which we see,
Time ticks on incessantly
And the clock on the wall cannot see at all.

For us, time pauses,
Ignoring progress, process, being.
In all the world the wheel still turns
And the blackbird is not sad.

Pamela Rollin

DAY OUT

The beach,
Gold crescent of grit,
Entices the family
With the season's call
To enjoy.

The picnic,
Created in haste
For the pleasure rare of eating
Beneath the clearing sky
Of blue.

The car,
Bulging with excitement -
Grey clouds drifting in its wake
From a noisy exhaust -
Gathering speed.

The bucket,
Clutched in the boy's hand,
Instrument of construction.
Anticipation huge:
Then rain.

Annie Harris

HOPE

Though the sky is overcast
Above it's always blue
Even when the thunder roars
Beyond it's always calm
When the fog is all around
Nearby the air is clear
Every time the rain pours down
Somewhere close is dry

Though my mind is overcast
Deep within there is some blue
Even when my heartbeat roars
Beyond is always calm
When the fog enshrouds my soul
Nearby my spirit's clear
Every time life's pouring down
Somewhere close is dry

Martin Hackett

POLITICS

Everyone prays for peace
As hopes become forlorn
Unless all conflicts cease
Many more will mourn

Talk with good intentions
Words uttered to deceive
Positive gestures and abstentions
Too difficult to believe

Pressured on both sides
On who can they rely?
Behind principles everyone hides
Disciples of peace decry

Suggestions of a compromise
Though proposed with grace
Found no one to sympathise
For fear of losing face

While many innocents die
Millions watch and wait
Life is passing by
Blinkered leaders contemplate

A W Day

TO LOVE SOMEONE

As I say so I love you
butterflies in my stomach
I can't hold them inside
I know it's love
it's only and only ever will
be one-way love
Why I feel a little down today
when it comes down to it
I know it's ever only
my fantasy
These feelings are so overwhelming
it really is hopeless love
it's hurting so deep it's making me weak
I know it's only my fantasy.

Sharon McHugh

MOURNING AFTER THRILLS

Seductiveness innocence
Of a little black dress
A mere array concealing
Hidden secrets
Expressing confused emotions -
The simple passing of life,
The endearing creation of one.
A simple disguise masking its value
Hurling torture
And apologetic.
The value of menace.
Yet the sweet, simple barer
Swinging hips, fully blossomed body
Arouses attention. Ingenuously.

Karishma Brahmbhatt

HE'LL BE THERE

You think,
        he won't be there
              to help you,
              but he will.

He will do the best he can,
        that is until,
              you look up
              and smile and say,
Now, I'm going on my way,
So he won't let you down,
He'll be there.

So no matter what you do,
        he will always
              see you through.
You might not think
        that this is true
But he'll be there.

E B Holcombe

HATRED

Conflicts rage across the line,
Anger manifests into taking of lives,
Bitter children whose innocence is lost,
Play games of war,
But games they are not,
Civilised civilians with hate in their eyes,
Fight for their Gods and their ways of life,
Sense lost in senselessness,
Reason removed from their minds
Hatred hunts so peace must die.

Nigel J Mason

ESCAPE

he didn't know how long he'd been running
only that he had to keep on moving
no time to rest, no time to take stock

he couldn't bring himself to look back
and yet he was scared of looking forward
he felt trapped, trapped where he was

his mind full of contradictions
he was surrounded by space
and yet felt claustrophobic

still he ran on, onwards at speed
never stopping, never looking back
he had to get away

what was he running from?
he couldn't tell
all that he knew was that he couldn't stop

all around him a terrible noise
everything so busy
so difficult to concentrate

he was tired now, so tired
all his energy drained
feeling so weak

what would happen if he stopped?
would it be so bad?
he couldn't even remember what he was running from

gradually he slowed, slowed to a stop
and then it dawned on him
the only thing he was running from was himself

Andy Sweet

THANATOS AND EROS

I am the dank, dark whiff of fear,
that sits beside you on the bus.
The foam-flecked, spluttering lunatic,
the febrile breath, the pus.
I am the stillborn, breech-birthed infant,
in a plastic carrier bag.
Despoiler of the fecund maid,
defender of the hag.
I ignite the choking incense,
blown through priestly robes and prattle.
I am the gargoyle on the roof,
that pouts your farewell rattle.

You are the ear pressed to the grille,
a wad of blotting paper.
Cupped pink on my atrocity,
lit by the candle's taper.
The embodied, living crucified,
lashed blood-raw with each transgression.
The dead, the done, the shat-upon,
each stinking, foul confession.
As like pins into a poppet
from a vengeful, angry fist,
each dissection, every slash and slice
is added to your list.

Would you were I.

Would I were you.

Would flesh to bone to dust.

Presenting id and ego,
we are the drivers of this bus.

P Hughes-Wilson

YOUTH'S LAMENT

We dip pale fingers
Into the pool
Of vague, nameless desire;
We reach out to feel the smouldering
Of a spiritual fire . . .

We knock, with bruising fingers
On the hard door of success -
But the door is slow to open
- And the effort growing less . . .

We are bewildered
By the cults and epithets around;
Out of the mould of childhood now
Our walls are not so sound . . .

Where is the God we cry out to
When we have lost the way?
- The golden heroes of our youth
It seems, have feet of clay . . .

The future is an unknown path
- So many dreams and goals;
With endless days
- So many ways
To lose our hearts - and souls . . .

Catherine L Woodward

UNTITLED

I must be here for some purpose
I know not why.
I am born to suffer,
Not to wither and die.

Death is final -
It sounds nice.
Take the chance.
Don't think twice.

My life has no meaning.
It's boring and flat.
I can't get out of the house,
So that settles that.

I know I have my animals,
And I do nothing to
Hurt them.
But I'm fed up with living
So what am I waiting for then?
Cowardice
Pure and simple.
I have tried many times
To take my life.
But I always end up
Staying alive.

Maxene Huntley

MEMORY

I will come to you.
In the labyrinth of mist
That rises from damp earth.
Sprinkling webs with diamonds.
Pointing wraithlike fingers at the sun.
The pearls of dew on rosebud transcends
All thoughts of sorrow.
Night has melted,
And I will come

Not in the purple haze of pain-wracked nights
Stumbling through Hades Halls
In morphined oblivion,
Where tears unceasing fall.
I am not there where waking has no part.
Regrets, apologies you will not find me there.
But in the pale half light of dawn.
You may search for me,
And I will come.

Margaret King

WATERFALL OF TEARS

Waterfall of tears flow across empty years
As a cloud of empty thoughts float amongst the
                               emptiness of broken hearts
As sad and lonely faces hide behind the clown's mask
That hides the pain of years of sorrow and sadness
And all we do is just laugh, laugh and laugh
At the clown's painted face of sorrow and despair.

Michael Spittles

ONE AFTERNOON

As the hill I climb, I can hear a church clock chime - there is green land
all around and, apart from the wind, there is no sound
Yellow wild flowers abound and cows and horses graze the ground
In the distance there are some vines, heavily laden with grapes -
all kinds.

A sign reads 'come in and try our wine' and, in a setting so sublime
with the perfume of sweet peas and thyme, a glass, or maybe two! will
suit me fine and I will bide my time before continuing with my climb.

Heather Moore

UNTITLED

Metallic to the taste
A life to waste
An amorphous star
Has carried me far
And here I stand
Guilty and afraid
Before beauty
A thundered reflection
Shuddering in and out of time
A fragile moment deafened
Living lost in this city
Where there is no night or day
Just the incessant rumble of trains
And the bitterness of loss
Incomplete
There is no joy
A spinning top
A useless toy
A bloodless sacrifice
Into the air

Chris Lodge

HERITAGE RAP

From the centre/ of a Linkway bridge
I can see the new town/ taking shape
Or at least the old town/ on its way
To vie for middle England -

Large traffic islands/ interlink
And almost form/ an Olympic flag
As multi-coloured/ retail parks
Create the New Jerusalem.

Though the sluggish green canal/ remains
And pays its tribute/ to all them -
To all the people/ entertained -
With nights and days of wracking phlegm -

The coal and glass and/ chemical phlegm
That caused the battle/ lost the wars -
But earned respect/ from all the dead
Though only in Scarlet-Ribbon songs -

So let this churlishness/ subside
And gather to/ embrace the new -
Come, let's all walk/ hand in hand
Across the bridge to wonderland.

Stephen Bonney

WIND ON THE WATER

It was only the wind
On the water,
But I'd hoped it was rain.
For I had yearned to recapture
By its mimic of tears
All the rapture
Of old irremediable pain.

It was only the wind
On the water,
An error of seeing, and yet
I treasure that prompt of deception
For touching the web
Of conception
Which summons recall of Kismet.

Dean Juniper

SENIOR MEMBERS

A curate is praying for our senior members'
midweek meeting, 'Help them to seek the kingdom
of God.' Our need may be greater than yours,
young man, but 'them' will become 'us' much sooner
than you think: when you find yourself adjusting
the distance of your book; asking what's said
to be repeated more than once; or wondering
why on earth you have clambered up the stairs!

As for me, I'm aware I tend to panic
with stuck-together bags at supermarkets;
or to dust the same thing twice, or to take
ages on the bus sorting out my purse,
both my hands manacled with entangled shopping,
or a dripping, half-collapsed umbrella,

not to mention the humiliation
of being shouted at on the phone by staff
of the health insurance, because I kept
mishearing the threshold sum for my physio:
her strong regional accent didn't help, either.

There's no end to listing our infirmities
until we reach a stage when we shut up.
Then may God help us and you, too, young man!

Michiko Matthews

THE PIANO

I am dumb
to say
myself.
This voice chirps, careless
                    like a sparrow
when inside
          I
am a dove, doe-eyed -
cooing to you.

Come, I mean
when Go, I say
Stay - I care - I think I love you
comes, I dare you to think - I need you

These fingers are stiff, gnarled, stumpy
to tell -
afraid.
This face - dull, pallid, ugly
to mirror,
mismade.

I know I'm strange
but caged
and cooped,
a screaming mute
I shout myself out of
                    dark depths;
bubbling sound in
quiet bursts
breaking
          the
                    surface.

Mickey Gough

APRÈS UN RÊVE

It may well be that when some time has passed
And all the pain and hurt that once was mine
Has somewhat eased, the day will come at last
When I shall think of you and not repine.
 My heart will remember and I'll be glad
 For all the happiness that once we had.

Until that time has come, the tears will fall
When e'er I hear your footsteps passing by
And know that you have gone on down the hall
And my world will be silent as I cry.
 I'll pray that you'll come back into my life
 And we'll have no more arguments or strife.

I think again about that dreadful day
When you decided we should meet no more.
You took my love and threw it all away
Not caring how I felt, you never saw
 How from that time it seemed my heart had gone
 And in its place was left a heavy stone.

To protest and entreaty you were deaf
We had to part - on this you were intent.
I gave you tears for they were all I'd left
And then, and then my love was all but spent.
 But still there is a corner in my soul
 Where I shall keep you safe - unknown to all.

And so I go on now from day to day
Knowing as each one passes, time will heal
And that eventually I shall say
I'm over you and no more will I feel
 That a day without you is lost in time,
 I shall look forward - and the wounds will bind.

Pam Love

THE YEAR OF OUR LORD - 2002

In this the year two thousand and two
The world where we live is better by far
Than it was when we entered it long ago
Housing and living conditions improved
And no one is starving, not even the poor
Not where *we* live at least.

It's good that this little part of the world
Had vision, endeavour, and worked to ensure
Each family has space to sleep, bathe and eat
And somewhere to think and reflect
Somewhere to pray for the rest of the world
For those less blessed than us.

But what of the floods, the fires and disasters
The trains and the planes and the cars that are crashing
The drugs and the thugs and the children gone missing
All in our part of the world
What of all this I hear you say
In the year of our Lord - 2002.

Have we forgotten in all our endeavour
To love one another and help our neighbour
Omitted to do what we ask others to do
In the pursuit of a better world
Have we forgotten to be the best of all
A friend to suffering humanity?

Is the year of the Lord, 2002?

Opal Innsbruk

THE WINDY PRECIPICE

High upon a windy precipice in my darkest hour
I long to feel a warm breeze or cool April shower
A heart pumped with fear, my eyes begin to sting
There is nothing in this place, not a single living thing

I scan the angry sky hoping a chink of light I will find
Dark clouds carry the sickness that wreaks havoc on my mind
I steel myself to look down half blind with heart-felt tears
Into total darkness that robs my precious living years

I beat a hasty retreat within, for a welcome place to hide
To find the emptiness there is crueller than any outside
A mind so very tired, muscles frozen, a body heavy and stiff
I find it hard to summon the energy to simply sob and sniff

What is this hell on earth, what path that led me here?
Stripped of my dignity and even my last frozen tear
Destined to my fate it seems my mind unable to cope
My tortured soul cries out for hope

To save this spirit breaking, I look within my heart
I find a small gift and pray we never part
I cling to hope with all my strength and beg her not to go
To save me from the darkness that pulls from below

Evil without end, I wonder should I jump after all
I fear one day I may be pushed, unable to avoid the fall
I trudge the wasteland inside hopeful I will find
A way off the windy precipice that exists inside my mind

Denise Startin

WHO'D FEED THE CATS?

The lonely old lady
Waits till I pass by
'Get me the peas dear, I'll fall if I try'

Another exchange, the second this week
Maybe her last chance to hover and speak.

I pass down the peas, and know now to linger
She twisted the ring on her wedding finger

She told me her sister had asked her to stay
But who'd feed the cats, while she was away?

The woman, I knew, was filled full of pride
All of her friends left, when her husband died.
Her sister's so kind, she'd asked her to stay
But who'd feed the cats if she went away?

I smile and I listen, and nod to her voice
I feel I must stand there, I've simply no choice
Her words start flowing
I began not to hear
The sense of her loneliness had filled me with fear.

Why is this woman, so desperate to speak?
Another exchange, my second this week.
Can she tell no one her feelings inside?
This fragile old lady, so full with pride.

Her sister 'Spoils the cabbage'
She lets it boil dry.
Something inside of me wanted to cry

I ask her quite plainly
'Are you going there today?'
But who'd feed the cats if she went away?

Lindsey Susan Powell

SLIGHTLY DIFFERENT, BUT STILL
JUST ANOTHER CHRISTMAS

Coal fire, carols, a cracked egg
Brussels sprouts waiting in a bucket

Long walks in the woods
Heard of a boy in a T-shirt who froze in the snow
A man threw-up in a private garden
There is red tinsel all over the floor

My anger -
I just want to go away
Be still in some medieval place
A pub lunch, a nice fire
Some brandy

Detachment - *'I don't really care'*
So leave my messy, cramped space
'Going to ground is the best thing'
Said a friend; cosiness is a myth.

A time then maybe to think
How to be an improvement on your parents
Learn from their mistakes
So you need no longer fall into the abyss

I called my sister in her faraway place
She rattled on
Then a friend in Bristol rang
And I *wanted* him to rattle on

I didn't want the stars and lights
The mince and songs
And certainly not cheery people
Sending token cards and gifts. Leave me alone
Somewhere mostly silent
Except for waves foaming on the honest shore

Karen Eberhardt Shelton

BEYOND THE HAIRSTYLE

Look beyond the hairstyle
and you will see the person -
beyond the pink and purple
beyond the poise, the pose
to eyes in repose.
Look twice not once
look straight look true
look with the real you
beyond the bounce and flounce
the flaunting and the hiding
beyond the persona the mask
the paint and the mascara
to the beautiful person
inside.

Stella Durand

ANCHOR FREE

Don't drop the anchor here my dear
Don't stop and bother me
Just lift it up and sail away
Across the bright blue sea.
And when the blue sea turns to grey
And storms around you bound
Remember, keep the anchor up
Don't drop it to the ground.
The sand is soft and will not hold
To make you feel secure
So sail away be far and free
Just don't come back
To bother me.

Constance Roper

ALONE

All day alone, I'm sorry and warm love
But, in the evening, only the fumes of thick smoke and silence
                                            reach your ear.
The glass wall across the table becomes thicker and more opaque as
                                            you rush at your kipper
Delving
And I tear at something or other
Searching
with huge disinterest, the disinterest of fear
Full on very little, a balloon of hot air.

Then it's coffee and my hot tears - the mints are off - and Mozart.
You listen to the oboe - caressed by the cool instrument and you
                                            fade away
Drifting
You open your eyes occasionally, only to shut them tight in bed.

The 'What's wrong?' comes too late for replies or touch.

J Redfearn

FATHER

You gave me red wellingtons
when I was five.
I wore them every day.

Would have slept in them if I could.
You said you'd come back for me.
I waited, wearing red wellingtons

- a beacon to guide you.
But I grew too big,
and had to throw them away.

Dawn Voice-Cooper

FROM WHERE?

Where did you say you hail from?
What was that name you said?
Many's the time, I'm asked to repeat the name again
Do you have it now? Has it finally sunk into your head?

It's actually quite famous, in its own little way.
Alright, it's no 'big city' with its own airport.
The sculptor and artist, Henry Moore, is the town's most famous sort.
My own doctor's surgery, proudly bears his name.
From humble beginnings, he rose up to much acclaim.
Thankfully, the streets he grew up in are no longer quite the same.

Let's not forget the town's own Vivian Nicholson
A pools winner from a long time ago.
Her infamous cries of 'Spend, spend, spend!'
Enjoyed her fame and fortune she did
Till the money ran out and came to a sad, sorry end.
But a recent West End show entitled the very same,
Reaped new revenues for our Viv
Enabling her (if she so wishes) to spend, spend, spend,
Once more, all over again.

Of course one mustn't forget its bingo halls,
'I only wanted such and such a number'
Is always spoken within its walls.
Feeling quite faint, becoming most irrational
All at the prospect of winning bingo's very own National.

Keep away from the jungle, our town's
Rugby League club's name.
If you're a 'Leed's Rhino' or a 'Bradford's Bull'
The Tigers can maul you on certain days.
Steeped in Rugby League glory.
Every old man you may speak to,
Has his own particular rugby story.

This once mainly coalmining, proud little town
Sadly the pits are no more, gone, been shut down.
Ever-changing landscapes, but not quite left all alone
We're soon to have our very own 'Snowdome'.

So much one could say about the place where I live,
Its colourful history, proud folk, some are quite sporty.
An oddball collection, mixture, a very strange horde
The town I try to describe
My town is *Castleford.*

Susan Barker

ELUSIVE BALLERINA

How gently she descends
     At first
Baring her gifts
     For the flowers
          New life
For me also
Proceeding
     To dance
          In the street
               Below
Her heavy perfume
     In the wake of
Beckoning for me
     To become her partner
Alas
     I can, but only
          Follow in sequence
Never able to embrace her
For she is this elusive ballerina
     The rain.

Sarah A O'Leary

DARK CLOUD

I fear there lies within me
A dark cloud across my soul
Black Orchids bloom
Within the gloom
Of my heart's tomb
Dark angry shadows
Bang, crash and clatter
Multiple voices
Gibber and chatter
About things that do
But then don't really matter
Terrible spirits
Spit forth strange rhyme
Used to be occasional
Now it's all the time
Sitting at my shoulder
Is a most frightening figure
Grinning and gurning
Through twisted tomb-stone teeth
Fetid shitty breath
Reeking of death
Positively bathing in its
Own awful wickedness
And when the devil lurches forward
Plants his stinking kiss
Upon my tortured lips
My tired and broken soul
Screams with the agony
Of shattered, scattered dreams
Whilst my new black heart
Thunders quickly
And then very slow . . .

Philip Gustard

BEDTIME WITH DAD

At my bedtime
my dad faced by a lion in Africa turned his back contemptuously
and the lion threw him down, jaws slavering red and open
teeth razor-white sharp
but my dad thrust his hand into those jaws down its throat
and through a slithery inner belly to the root of its tail
then with one gigantic heave he turned it inside out,
that's what he said.

At my bedtime
my dad saved a white mermaid at Blackpool from an octopus
by tying it in knots
and that same day saved a black mermaid from a shark
by forcing cod liver oil down it with a bicycle pump
he happened to be carrying
upon which the shark was violently sick on the seabed
and took no further interest,
that's what he said.

At my bedtime
my dad put his thumbs into his mouth and blew
and blew until his biceps swelled like balloons.
He once saved his life at sea by using them to keep afloat.
I tried to blow mine up but couldn't.
There'll come a time,
that's what he said.

At his own last bedtime
lions and mermaids waiting his arrival
he gave me a morning - clean shaven kiss and
'Be a good boy'
is what he said.
I was sixty-three.

K Baldwin

THOR

The summer evening sky glows.
Buildings, with shapes of shadows,
Lights and shades, form near twilight
Landscapes.

In the village, my companions, who I
Would share my last loaf with, and I,
The cluttered day falling away from us,
Head for posh pubs -
The Black Bull, The Red Lion and
The Old White Bear.

As we sit, joking, laughing and
Drinking golden brown bitter from pint glasses,
I notice that the sun's empire is dwindling.

Small birds, that flitter and hide in bushes,
Notice that the sun is descending.

I, alcohol-stung, become more and more
Sluggish.

At midnight, we stagger off to our homes
Singing Cole Porter to cautious cats.

David M Garnett

THE FISH

Taking me to places
far beyond my
most extravagant
dreams, and my
insufficient means,
I would not keep my
Goldfish in a bowl.

Let him sink, or learn
to swim; that's what
fishes do, right?
Let my heart
continue to loudly
sing. Don't take away
my Goldfish credit card.

Paula Puddephatt

THE CHIEFTAIN

When weed and wine,
And love combine
In springtime, Maya's evenin',
T'ward Gaia's promised summertime
When seein' is believin';
And the Chieftain calls
Through grey stone walls
'Break your embrace, I'm grievin!

Come see the horse and rider
Leap the moonlit sea
Come hear the fiddler break
You through
Come leave your ring with me.'
Then hear the fiddler's fading note,
As, arm in arm,
Through freedom's farm,
We skip and stride back home.

Where weed and wine
And love combine;
Eve's night-time now is day,
'Tis Gaia's promised summertime
In your embrace I stay.

Bill Brierley

JOINED BY RITES OF WISDOM

Libran star rising
Through incense smoke they drift
Angel voice broke crying
Their muted love we sift
Taurean wandering rogue
Beyond her twilight dream
On the threshold of awakening
Roaming on the stream
They mystify my Neptune
Upon it they are one
Joined by rites of wisdom
Beneath the seldom sun.

S Grayson

SON AND MOON

full moon
splintered
by silhouette
of tree
barbed wire
bouquet
glinting
mournfully
crown of thorns
adorns the
suffering face
of Christ
but cannot
snuff the light
burning from
the Son of
the Holy One

Alex Warner

OLD WORLD - NEW WORLD

She looked out the window,
And there stood a man.
His face was withered,
He held out his hand.

He called for her aid,
But she could not hear.
His time has passed,
Her own stood near.

Standing not on our earth,
But on his own,
Dangling mid-air,
His layer had worn.

Her doubting eyes,
At him still shone,
As she watched him vanish,
Back to his home.

Angela Helen

YOU

I used to let myself be torn apart
Habitually crying for the death of my heart
With muddled thoughts I clung to you
So much shame I blamed on you
All my pain was caused by you
And all the tears I cried for you
My every thought controlled by you
All my scars because of you
I no longer lay the blame with you
Because I let you

Kelly Cortés

CAR BOOT

Once carefully arranged, dusted regularly, they stood
on an old Welsh dresser.
In the room that was Sunday best, and
visitors only.
That smelt of shut windows and faint mustiness.
But they knew they were loved - though a trifle lonely.
Now with the fumes of fish and chips, burgers, and
sizzling onions nearby,
A cheap wooden stand is their resting place.

Children in bright crayon colours dash by -
Bargain hunters of the future, learning to make their
coins go far.
Yesterday's marbles with squiggly patterns and
gobstopper sizes, are favourites,
So too Enid Blyton, jigsaws, and the famous
Dinky car.
Mothers find succulent strawberries and non-stringy beans.
Plus home-made cakes, they've no time to bake anymore.

'Save you packing up, I'll give 'a pony' for
this little lot.'
Startled by the loud voice, they recognise the rough arm
That had turned each one upside down before.
'Which one of us is valuable?' They tremble
'Others he'll harm.'
With a sigh, the stallholder agrees, saving one to
remember his mother.
The trader's face falls a mile - and their question
is answered.

Mary Jelbart

OVER THE TOP

Splish, splash, splish, splash
Thick gooey slimy mud
Cold, wet, alone
What have I done?
Splish, splash, splish, splash
Black fat bodies, long thin tails
Razor sharp teeth, bright eyes
Rats, rats fear.
Splish, splash, splish, splash
Dirty, tired, hungry
Rat-a-tat-tat, go the guns
Thump, thump, thump, beats my heart
Splish, splash, splish, splash
Watch your step - over the top
Walk - don't run
Mind the wire
Splish, splash, splish, splash
Bullet, blood, pain
All fall down
Sorry Mother
Splish, splash, splish, splash

Katy Holderness

SUBMISSIONS INVITED
SOMETHING FOR EVERYONE

POETRY NOW 2003 - Any subject,
any style, any time.

WOMENSWORDS 2003 - Strictly women,
have your say the female way!

STRONGWORDS 2003 - Warning!
Age restriction, must be between 16-24,
opinionated and have strong views.
(Not for the faint-hearted)

All poems no longer than 30 lines.
Always welcome! No fee!
Cash Prizes to be won!

Mark your envelope (eg *Poetry Now) 2003*
Send to:
Forward Press Ltd
Remus House, Coltsfoot Drive,
Peterborough, PE2 9JX

OVER £10,000 POETRY PRIZES TO BE WON!

Judging will take place in October 2003